THE I

Your Efforts Are Always Rewarded

ATIF KAMRAN

Serial Entrepreneur, Business Strategist

International Trainer and Inspirational Speaker

www.TheEffortBank.com

Kemp House
152-160 City Road
London, EC1V 2NX
United Kingdom

ISBN: 978-1-917003-73-5

Published by Atif Kamran and Action Wealth Publishing.
Printed and bound in the United Kingdom

Although the author and publisher have made every effort to ensure the accuracy and completeness of information contained in this book, we assume no responsibility for errors, inaccuracies, omissions, or any inconsistency herein. Any slights on people, places, or organisations are unintentional.

The material in this book is provided for educational purposes only. No responsibility for loss occasioned to any person or corporate body acting or refraining to act as a result of reading material in this book can be accepted by the author or publisher.

Mirza Ghulam Muhammad

To my father, the pillar of strength and integrity in my life. Your unwavering commitment to hard work, honesty, and family values has shaped me into the person I am today. It is because of your guidance and example that I have embarked on this journey of writing *The Effort Bank*. Your legacy lives on through the principles you instilled in me, and this book is a tribute to the lessons you taught me.

Your dedication to honouring your commitments and never giving up, even in the face of adversity, has been a source of inspiration for me. Your tenacity and perseverance have been the driving force behind my own pursuit of success. As I share the knowledge and insights I have gained over the years in entrepreneurship and leadership, I do so with gratitude for the foundation you laid for me.

Through *The Effort Bank,* I hope to honour your memory and the values you passed down to me. Your belief in the power of hard work, determination, and family bonds has been the cornerstone of my life's journey. This book is a testament to the impact you have had on shaping my character and guiding me towards my goals. Thank you, Dad, for being my guiding light and the reason behind this book.

CONTENTS

ACKNOWLEDGMENTS

ACKNOWLEDGING THE GIANTS I have had the privilege to learn from over the past two decades is essential. The attitudes, knowledge, and skills I have acquired from other successful individuals have been instrumental in shaping my understanding and development of the concept of the Effort Bank.

Their wisdom and guidance have been invaluable in helping me navigate the world of entrepreneurship and leadership, and I am grateful for the lessons they have imparted.

INTRODUCTION

DO YOU EVER WONDER why some individuals achieve great success with minimal effort, and others who put in significant effort fail to reach their desired outcomes?

The quest to find answers led me to create the concept of the Effort Bank. I realised that making an impact doesn't require a monumental act. Instead, small steps are enough to build confidence through small wins, as every incredible journey begins with a single step.

Imagine that a piggy bank was given to you on the day you were born. With each stride and endeavour you made in life, savings were added to the piggy bank. This ever-expanding piggy bank sitting beside your bed doesn't contain money. However, it is indeed a bank—an Effort Bank. An Effort Bank isn't a physical bank; instead, it's a personal vault of experiences gained through the investment of your hard work.

As you grew, you learned to walk. It was worth it, as not only did it enable you to grab cookies from the counter, but it also put coins in the Effort Bank. Learning to speak was even more valuable, allowing you to communicate with your loved ones. Additionally, mastering reading and writing was unquestionably beneficial, providing access to knowledge and the world around you. And in each of those experiences, your piggy bank grew because of your effort.

It doesn't matter whether you label your childhood and experiences as 'good' or 'bad.' We all possess a unique tale an assortment of experiences. Some experiences are uplifting, while others may leave much to be desired.

In your everyday activities, consider each action as depositing a coin into your personal savings bank. For instance, maybe you had to revise your budget three times before getting it right – that's a coin added to your bank. Or, you might have collaborated with a new group of individuals and faced some difficulties – that's another coin in the bank. Regardless of how complex, stressful, or overwhelming your efforts are, you will eventually be rewarded for them, if not immediately, then later.

What is clear is that reflecting on your daily approach and thoughts about your actions is vital. Life is marked by constant and fluctuating rhythms and cycles, with moments of stability followed by periods of turbulence. And if you don't deposit enough into your Effort Bank, there will come a time when you need to withdraw from it, only to discover that the balance is not adequate.

Gaining the ability to identify, respect, and accept the negative and positive cyclical shifts we undergo can enable us to live and lead our lives from a position of personal empowerment. Yet, to do it effectively, you need to understand your Effort Bank's role in life entirely.

As an entrepreneur, I've spent much of my life coaching people on business strategies. I thrive off helping entrepreneurs and leaders reach their life objectives by offering personal and professional development training. My work energises me and gives me a sense of purpose, as there's no greater fulfilment than teaching others the value of cultivating their Effort Bank.

In my younger years, I believed that to achieve something significant, you had to aim for something grand. I thought meaningful actions were only carried out by prominent, iconic leaders and philanthropists.

But then I heard a story.

During a storm, a man strolled along the beach as the sea hurled numerous fish onto the shore. The man attempted to pick up a pair of fish at once and toss them back into the water, but every time he did so, another 50 would land on the beach.

His friend observed his actions, puzzled by the seemingly futile effort. He asked the man why he bothered to throw two fish back into the ocean when 50 more were washed ashore simultaneously.

The man acknowledged his friend's point. He explained that while it may look counterproductive, each time he saved two fish, it made a difference. The cumulative impact would be significant if fish were continually thrown back into the water.

The narrative closely mirrors my own life experiences. As I journeyed around the world, accumulating wisdom and insights, I encountered numerous individuals from diverse backgrounds.

This book explains this phenomenon through what I learned from my life experiences and provides strategies for becoming one of the fortunate few who attain greatness. In it, I will guide you towards a more profound comprehension of your unique Effort Bank, enabling you to manage it more effectively so that when it comes, you have ample savings to cash out.

It's true. We were all given that Effort Bank at birth. It is a bank within everyone's grasp. Yet it's crucial to learn how to manage it to make deposits and withdrawals that yield more significant long-term benefits.

PART I:

DEPOSITING INTO THE EFFORT BANK

THE CONCEPT OF AN Effort Bank reminds us not to focus on the result but to work hard persistently. It emphasises the importance of acting rather than dwelling on the outcome.

Frequently, our efforts are influenced by the potential outcome, determining how much energy we invest, which shouldn't be the case. I want to emphasise the importance of setting goals and targets, but the key is to let go of concerns regarding the outcome.

For instance, I was on a call with a friend the other day when another call came through. Someone was contacting me for assistance as they faced some business challenges. I politely told my friend I would call him back after helping this person, which took about an hour. The caller was an entrepreneur who started their venture last year and sought my advice on various matters, even asking for connections. When I called my friend back, he wondered how much I earned from that call, knowing that I am a business consultant and I charge for my time. I hadn't made any money from it. I explained that sometimes, I genuinely want to help others without expecting anything in return, as my long-term goal is to guide people in making money. I believe in the concept of 'what goes around, comes around,' and I know that if I do good deeds, someone will help me when needed.

Through my experiences, I know that acts of kindness are coins deposited into my Effort Bank and carried forward. Throughout our lives, we'll experience moments of triumph and accomplishment and instances where we fall short. However, does that imply we should disregard our efforts and dedication? Should failure be seen as a sign of inadequacy? This prevalent mentality leads us to excessively celebrate victories and harshly criticise ourselves when faced with failure. Unfortunately, this overlooks the hard work we invest in pursuing our objectives and fails to consider the learning experience from our unsuccessful attempts.

Too often, the effort is undervalued because it's not as tangible as accomplishments, which have clear benchmarks for success. But does that mean effort isn't as crucial as the outcome?

Consider this: we might reward our kids with a special meal for ranking first in their class, but what if they put in extra time to stay after school and discuss the lesson with their teacher? Their effort might not make them the top performer, but it's still worth celebrating!

Similarly, failure doesn't mean it's the end of the world. Instead of criticising our children for failing, why not help them focus on the learning experience and determine what went wrong and how to improve it? Rather than saying, 'You're not good enough for this, that's why you failed,' we could ask, 'What did you learn from this experience, and how can I assist you with this?' By shifting our perspective on effort and re-evaluating how we view failure, we can help our children navigate life more meaningfully, so they are better equipped for adulthood.

CHAPTER ONE

HUMBLE BEGINNING

OVER TIME, TODAY'S society has become addicted to the tiny bursts of dopamine we get from social media likes, sophisticated makeover tools, and social filters, causing us to yearn for immediate results with little work. This mindset has seeped into almost every aspect of our lives, from fad diets to businesses promising instant success. However, these accomplishments tend to be elusive, intangible, or, at the very least, extremely delicate. If our progress and achievements aren't based on a solid foundation of effort, clarity in our path, and consistency, they can easily shatter at the slightest hint of doubt.

A solid foundation of hard work is crucial, as even the slightest issue can destroy our achievements. Just look around – the instability of what we once considered stable has collapsed. Those who already had strong working habits in place have reaped the rewards. It's about understanding the importance of dedication and maintaining it consistently.

Acknowledging the significance of our daily decisions can be challenging when we're bombarded with messages that make us question if our hard work is in vain.

However, that's far from the truth.

A Strong Family Unit

I hail from a quaint little town named Khushab, nestled in the heart of Pakistan, with around 50,000 residents. It's a modest town, and I can't help but share a bit about it as I take immense pride in my roots there. The moniker 'Khushab' is derived from two Persian terms, 'khush' and 'aab', signifying 'sweet' and 'water'. The town's name certainly has a charming ring to it.

When the Persians arrived in this region, they discovered the water was sweet and nourishing. They were smitten, and so were we. My district covers roughly 2,500 square miles, yet it boasts an incredible variety of landscapes. Imagine having mountains, picturesque valleys, lakes, waterfalls, fertile plains, deserts, and rivers within reach. It's like experiencing a little bit of everything you could ever desire.

It was an ideal setting to be raised in a solid family bond between myself and my three brothers, of whom I was the youngest. Our father worked as a mining engineer and was indeed a self-made individual. Through perseverance, he managed to provide us with a comfortable middle-class life. His greatest treasure was his children, as he invested in our education and upbringing instead of accumulating wealth. It was his deeds that instilled in all of us a solid and nurturing family environment.

Our hometown is also well-known for two delectable sweets – Dhoda and Patisa. Whenever we planned a trip to visit relatives in other cities, I recall how we were expected to bring signature Khushab sweets as gifts, and we felt pride. This gifting culture was always present, and growing up, I appreciated the emphasis on giving.

It was never about giving gifts because you felt obliged, but my brothers and I learned how incredible it felt to offer a gift that brought pure joy to another's face.

It didn't matter where my father went; everyone knew him and held him in high regard. He was a true gentleman. As a result, our family also enjoyed a good reputation within the community. When I visited new places, people often recognised me as Mirza Ghulam Muhammad's son, which led to preferential treatment.

Due to our age gap, I would occasionally accompany my elder brother, who served as a father figure to me. They all cared for me and instilled the core values that shaped my character. So, we would go out together, meet his friends, or attend various social events. He would then teach me proper etiquette, guiding me on what to do or avoid in certain situations and always explaining the reasons behind his advice. This provided me with valuable learning experiences.

At times, I would feel under pressure to abide by all these dos and don'ts to make sure that I upheld my family image. Yet, it was never a burden. I understood that when I was in certain situations, I needed to act in a specific manner as I was representing my family.

Witnessing my father's dedication first-hand inspired me to understand the significance of putting in effort from a young age. There is something gratifying about working relentlessly towards a goal, not just in the present moment but also for the future. Growing up in a nurturing and loving family environment was crucial in shaping my perspective on life.

One of the most valuable lessons I can recall learning from my father during my early years is honouring your commitments.

I recall hearing my family members, including my brothers, discussing a particular event at some point in our lives. I can't quite remember when it happened or how old I was then. My father had borrowed money from someone and promised to repay it by the last day of the month.

The person he borrowed from lived a couple of hours away by car. So, on the agreed-upon date, my father drove to their home to return the money. Surprised, the lender said, 'Wait a minute, why did you come all this way? I was planning to drive down to your place in a few days, and you could've given me the money then.'

But my father insisted, 'No, I told you I'd pay you back by the 30th. I had to make sure you got the money by then. I knew you'd be coming soon, but I wanted to keep my word.' And that is precisely the kind of man my father was. He always kept his word, no matter what.

Even today, I remember that conversation clearly, as it instilled in me the importance of keeping your word, particularly in financial matters. This has become a crucial aspect of my life. This value, which I learned from my father, has earned me the respect of many people. When you establish strong values, others notice and form an impression of you based on those principles. In my experience, this has been quite beneficial.

My father was self-employed, and his role in mining involved travelling to distant mountain locations to conduct surveys. Afterwards, he'd create intricate maps indicating where and at what angles and depths to excavate tunnels, maximising the mine's potential. He was considered an expert in his field and sought after.

He was ambitious and leased mining rights from the government in a mountain range. He initially thrived but eventually encountered a decline in coal reserves, leading to a loss. Despite this, he never surrendered. What I recall most about him is his tenacity. He wasn't satisfied with providing his specialised services for good pay; he continually pursued various businesses. This determination is something I've embraced in my own life, ensuring that I never give up either.

The outcomes we attain from our life experiences, such as my upbringing, frequently mirror the energy we invest in them. Naturally, everyone faces difficulties – that's expected. Obstacles? Absolutely!

Yet, it all boils down to us: are we prepared to work to learn, develop, transform, practice, and conquer – as my father did?

There will be days when we feel more exhausted than usual, and exerting that extra effort might be more challenging. But giving it your all every day is always worth it. Each decision matters, and we possess the power to make these choices at any given moment.

The Loss of Childhood

When my father passed away, he had been the primary provider. My mother was a housewife, and while my older brothers were working, they hadn't quite established themselves in their careers yet. Suddenly, we faced a financial crisis, but thankfully, my brothers stepped up to support the family – keeping the household running and contributing to my education.

However, our lifestyle inevitably changed, which shook me to my core. It served as a wake-up call, making me realise that until then, I had taken life for granted and didn't worry about the little things.

My dad was there, and he would do whatever was needed. His passing left me to grow up rather quickly. I often met new people who commented that I seemed more mature than my age. At the time, I didn't understand what they meant by that. Reflecting on it now, I know I missed out on many things other teenage kids were doing, such as recreational activities and trips. I was never part of those things. Having to grow up quickly left me feeling as though I always had to 'catch up', and even during my teenage, college and university years, my sole focus was on diligently working, studying, and laying the foundation for my career.

I was acutely aware of the current family's financial constraints, so when he passed, I quickly moved into a budget-friendly place during my studies. When I lived in a hostel, often during those times, my roommate and I would head to a restaurant, order a meal for one, and split it between us - to ensure we didn't exceed our budget. It was such a challenging stage in my life.

Challenging as those times were, I also learned so much. I discovered that instead of feeling bogged down by constantly needing to be perfect, it's better to focus on giving your all in everything you do.

I understood that life's most significant achievements don't just magically happen. Our most important accomplishments –truly memorable, joyous, monumental, transformative, and impressive – arise from our hard work.

Success in health, business, and relationships is an ongoing process that depends on our ability to make the right choices and consistently give our best effort. We must put our energy into everything we do, and it's equally important to learn from or celebrate the outcomes of our hard work. Ideally, we can experience both learning and celebration simultaneously, which motivates us to keep pushing forward with our efforts.

No matter who you are, your upbringing, or the lessons you learned, difficulties arise when we shift towards a more mindful way of living and depositing into our Effort Bank.

Perhaps you are in a position where your occupation isn't fulfilling your more significant goals, your daily habits aren't benefiting your well-being, or your relationships aren't making either party happy.

At some point in life, you must step back and wonder – hold on – are my actions harmful to me? Are the decisions I'm making leading me to what I truly desire?

Today, we tend to feel overloaded and too dedicated to our work. We are constantly bombarded with the concept of doing more, being more, and no matter how much you try, your endeavours are insufficient. Yet when you understand that the energy and effort you put in is an investment into your Effort Bank, the rewards can be fruitful.

For example, when I completed my degree in computer engineering, I landed my first job as a system engineer at a company in Islamabad, Pakistan. It was an exciting role, especially since it was my first real-world experience after my studies. The company hired a few other recent graduates as well, and during the initial three months, we didn't receive any salary since we were on probation and still in training. However, they committed to paying us a specific amount once the training period ended.

I devoted so much effort to that organisation, which was responsible for managing computer network systems in various banks and other critical locations. I performed so well that they entrusted me with overseeing an entire bank's computer system network – while I was still on probation. After three months, I inquired about my salary but received nothing. They kept saying the head office would send the funds, but nothing came.

I discovered that this was the company's routine every three months. Individuals come and go as they grow tired of waiting, and the company receives nothing short of free labour.

I could have gotten angry about this. After all, I had to travel and spend my money during probation. I was seriously out of pocket. However, despite their deception, I chose not to let it bother me too much. I decided to be thankful for the experience I gained, as the hands-on learning was much more than what I learned in university.

Instead, all the energy was deposited into my Effort Bank. And that reward was paid, as another position I applied for, I would not have gotten had it not been for the experience I gained during my probation period. My interviewees were so impressed that they offered me the job on the spot with a salary twice the market rate.

One thing I'm sure of is that by consistently putting in our best effort, we'll achieve results. Moreover, when we put forth our effort during the most challenging times, we might not always be thrilled with the outcome, but we'll feel better for giving it our all. There's significance in striving towards a goal and immense satisfaction in exerting ourselves.

The only caveat is that we must be present and appreciate the achievements.

Taking such steps throughout our lives helps us accumulate reserves in our Effort Bank. Even when confronted with obstacles, like when I was eventually let go from my second job, having enough money in our Effort Bank enables us to recover quickly.

What's truly remarkable is that consistently putting in the effort day after day eventually transforms it into a habit. We still enjoy the benefits, but what once required effort now feels effortless.

Now that you have a better understanding of how to deposit into your Effort Bank, I will discuss in the next chapter how it can work for you so that you don't find yourself in a situation where you need to withdraw only to discover there are no funds in the bank.

CHAPTER TWO

HOW THE EFFORT BANK WORKS

THE UNDERLYING PRINCIPLE of an Effort Bank is that when individuals engage in a task, they either achieve their goal or not, but their efforts are always rewarded sooner or later. Success brings immense joy, while failure often leads to disappointment. Many attribute their outcomes to luck, particularly when they fail. When these individuals fall short of success, they frequently consider themselves unlucky and envy the fortunate ones, primarily because they refuse to accept responsibility. They don't attribute their failure to something they did or didn't do and prefer to pin it on luck.

Eventually, they start to believe that their efforts are futile. After repeated failures, they minimise their input, assuming they will fail anyway.

Instead of giving the next venture everything they have, they decide to reduce their effort to 70%, thinking this will lessen their disappointment. Unfortunately, this leads to inevitable failure, reinforcing their belief that they will lose.

They then convinced themselves that it was wise to minimise their losses by not investing entirely in the task. This cycle continued, with their effort decreasing each time, leading to repeated failures.

This pattern of failure solidifies their belief in luck. They think success hinges on luck and resorting to superstitions or other means to attract good fortune. They fail to grasp the concept of the 'Effort Bank'.

The Effort Bank idea suggests that when you put in the effort, it's either rewarded or stored for the future. If your efforts are rewarded instantly, you succeed. If not, they are stored in your Effort Bank and will be rewarded later. When you understand and accept this, failure doesn't cause such sadness because your efforts are never wasted; they are stored for future success.

With that mindset, you'll realise the rewards will be more significant for all your efforts.

Today's individuals invest considerable time in taxing activities that yield no benefits, while others do less but accomplish more.

How is this possible?

If we break Effort Bank into three classifications, we can see how effort and commitment can eventually lead to value.

The first category of time is stimulus. This denotes time used to respond to what is thrust upon us and address matters that demand our attention. The realm of social media epitomises this: a world where everything is in constant motion, but nothing substantial is occurring. This is time spent replying to emails, responding to calls, answering inquiries, or attending meetings others have arranged.

In today's world, you must inevitably devote some time to responding to stimuli; in some job industries, it is a requirement. However, if responding isn't part of your job description, it's best to avoid spending time in this category as it will keep you in a perpetual cycle of reactions—which means you are not fulfilling your obligations.

There will always be a project that needs completion or a presentation that needs to be drafted. The more time you spend on 'stimuli,' the longer these tasks remain unattended.

You may be incredibly busy and fatigued, feeling deserving of more rewards for your exertion. Still, after all this time and energy spent reacting to stimuli, your obligations haven't lessened - they've escalated.

The second category of time is commitment, which refers to the moments when you engage in tasks that you have pledged to complete, fulfilling the needs of others. You consciously ignore all potential distractions to focus wholeheartedly on the work that needs to be completed.

The sensation of accomplishment is immense, and you have been highly productive during this time. The feeling of satisfaction is unparalleled as you now have a clear agenda.

However, this sense of achievement may be misleading as it doesn't necessarily alter the demands or distractions of the upcoming day. The subsequent day, you return to the same cycle that existed before you were in your commitment phase.

But you feel in control as your worries and remorse about what you 'ought to' do have been managed, allowing you to seek distractions to occupy your time leisurely.

Many people find themselves in a continuous loop, oscillating between the phases of 'stimuli' and 'commitment' of time throughout their lives.

The third category of time, where effort is banked, is precisely that: effort time. It signifies a rewarding phase since it's the juncture where you carve out your future. Mastering the intricacies of advanced time management involves skilfully manoeuvring through the stimulus phase, fulfilling your commitments, and then dedicating time to the effort segment.

This is when you undertake tasks that you either love or those that can alter your future. Completing these tasks can transform your business, time management, or life.

'Effort time' is not about mundane tasks like deleting or filing an email or responding to it. It's about making significant changes - actions that create a domino effect on your future.

Doing this paves the way for a transformed life, freeing up time for genuine leadership activities and success. But staying in the 'effort time' is crucial. And the more you do, the more it will feel like the new normal, even if it doesn't initially.

We're so accustomed to feelings of guilt or over-obligating ourselves that the emotions that are linked to 'effort time', such as pleasure, feel alien to us. Too often, if something makes us happy, we wrongly tell ourselves we shouldn't do it.

But this is where you should invest your time. The more effort you put into worthy aspects of yourself and your career, the more opportunity you will have to create something unique and live your dream. When working within 'effort time', you naturally tend to take on challenging tasks and relish them.

Aside from the practical aspect of not being ruled by stimuli or responsibility, the skill to achieve this is the emotional intelligence of time. It's about being at ease with emotions other than guilt or feeling overwhelmed. It's about embracing the enjoyment of your current activity and letting it drive you forward.

It's Where You Are Going

Reflecting on my children navigating their school years, engaging in various sports and extracurricular activities, and enjoying their time, it's clear that a world of possibilities awaits them once they venture into higher education and beyond. Yet, they remain unaware of these opportunities, a significant part of their journey.

I recall my own experiences during my university years. My accommodation was a small, cost-effective hostel two hours away from my hometown. I distinctly remember a time when there was a power outage in our hostel. My friend and I studied under the streetlight's glow with an exam scheduled for the following day. Those were challenging times that I often reminisce about.

I remember telling my friend that one day, we would look back at these experiences and share our stories of overcoming adversity to achieve our goals. And, indeed, we accomplished what we set out to do despite the hurdles we faced.

I firmly believe that through dedication and hard work, like my father, who hailed from a modest background, we all can succeed, regardless of our beginnings. It's about staying convinced that you have a place at the top.

A valuable piece of wisdom is, *"Don't judge your start by comparing it to the midpoint or conclusion of another's journey."*

Have you ever taken a moment to understand the modest beginnings and career trajectories of successful individuals? Were you aware that Steve Jobs was dismissed from the very company he started? Or that Michael Jordan didn't make his high school basketball team?

Every grand success narrative involves challenges.

Success stories are captivating for most people. We all aspire to our own degree of success and want to be in charge of writing that script.

However, if we consider the existing societal standards of success, only a handful can achieve it. And among these few, some have success handed to them. Don't get me wrong; there's nothing wrong with being born into wealth or prosperity or having a system that perfectly aligns with your goals. However, success is almost a given when someone gets a head start or hails from a prosperous lineage. When the odds are against someone, and they still triumph, their success story becomes inspiring.

For self-made people who start from scratch, quite literally or figuratively, what is interesting is the elements of their character that differentiate them from those who inherit their family's trade or wealth or those who marry into success. It would be best if you were keen to understand these elements that shape self-made successful individuals, even when starting from nothing.

Some prosperous individuals worldwide have never earned a degree, and some have never entered a university. A prime example is Richard Branson if you don't consider his Honorary Doctorate. These people are brilliant and cunning. It's a universal truth that everyone fumbles and errs. In some form or another, to some degree or another, we all stumble.

People who succeed starting from scratch may not necessarily commit fewer errors than the rest of us. Instead, they excel at learning from their positive and negative experiences, including missteps. Every mistake is a lesson banked in their Effort Bank, and they are fully aware of it.

Irrespective of whether they are high school dropouts or hold PhDs, they do not depend on textbooks or precede thinkers in their respective fields. They have a unique mindset, possibly because they dare to, but certainly because they are capable of it. They can think strategically, profoundly, rationally, and astutely. They scrutinise everything meticulously and swiftly, striving for meaningful solutions and understanding that the answers or outcomes might not come today.

Regardless of their intelligence, these self-made individuals maintain a grounded perspective. No matter how far they climb the ladder of success, they never lose touch with reality. This is not necessarily linked to the belief that their humble beginnings are unforgettable. Indeed, many self-made successful individuals share modest roots, but this is not what keeps them humble.

Instead, humility is an inherent quality in them. If these individuals had been born into wealth or success, they would likely still possess this trait. Their humility remains unaltered even as they achieve success. Therefore, humility is crucial in their journey toward success, starting from zero.

Intelligence combined with humility is a rare quality. This rarity empowers an individual to overcome hurdles and challenges. An intelligent, competent individual without humility would disdain menial tasks during tough times and fail to see the value of an Effort Bank. An intelligent individual needs humility to collaborate effectively with others who might struggle to keep pace with their advanced thinking. Even smart people don't know everything. They can also need assistance. It requires humility to seek and ask for help.

People who come from humble beginnings also tend to possess a strong sense of pride. It's important to distinguish between pride and arrogance or egotism. These individuals take pride in their work, the legacies they aspire to build, and their visions. As such, they refrain from dishonest practices and manipulation. They don't flatter others for personal gain or rely on others' achievements. They don't resort to unethical means to attain success.

Those who struggle to maintain their success often resort to unethical actions or rely on the achievements of others, but these do not contribute to their personal Effort Bank. Riding on the success of others ultimately leads to a lack of personal growth and fulfilment.

Self-made individuals are modest and may even serve coffee to their guests, yet they know their worth.

Expanding Knowledge and Skills

Education is crucial to our existence. Much like the way food fuels our bodies, ongoing education stimulates our minds. Engaging in lifelong learning is a critical instrument for everyone. In today's world, consistent learning plays a significant role in developing crucial thinking abilities and new ways to connect with individuals from various cultural backgrounds.

The idea of living without continuous learning is unimaginable.

There is a growing interest in enhancing general knowledge these days. The need to know more is a requirement of contemporary life, as many daily skills, such as problem-solving, communication capabilities, and open-mindedness, are rooted in a solid general knowledge foundation.

From a societal perspective, our personality is often evaluated by our knowledge level. It's challenging to be self-assured, articulate clear viewpoints, and leave a positive impression without a sound understanding of common knowledge.

Lifelong learning is a tool for keeping pace with the ever-evolving world. Enhancing general knowledge yields benefits in all aspects of life. It instils confidence, improves social abilities, and aids personal development and well-being. It forms the foundation upon which further learning can be built and banked.

Always remain receptive to learning and continue to expand your knowledge. By broadening your knowledge, you learn to accept that not everything is within your control. This is about embracing acceptance through learning.

It's important to remember that everything you learn from other people, what you read in a book, or what you hear on a podcast is information you can bank and use at another stage. Besides gaining new insights, reading or listening can also enhance your vocabulary. Further, it triggers several cognitive processes, including attention, concentration, understanding, and evaluation.

Microlearning is also an excellent tool for your Effort Bank and is geared towards equipping you with precise knowledge for addressing specific tasks in your professional or personal life. Its popularity has surged over recent years as it focuses on one topic and delivers information in manageable chunks. It eliminates unnecessary information, time wastage, and cognitive overburdening. Consequently, microlearning can bridge knowledge gaps, enhance your overall skill set, and aid in knowledge acquisition.

Broadening your knowledge isn't solely about what you internalise. Building connections is of utmost significance to me as a socially active individual. A vital part of social interaction involves narrating stories and explaining certain concepts to others. Your newfound knowledge can essentially become an exciting topic for discussion. Ample research indicates that memory improvement requires the brain to reproduce information. This process forms neurological links that safeguard the storage of knowledge. Hence, elucidating concepts to others enhances your reputation as a knowledgeable person and propels your intellectual growth.

You may have read about staying curious, and I firmly believe it is critical to continuous knowledge. This mindset opens a limitless world of opportunities for acquiring new and stimulating expertise. By fostering an ongoing curiosity, you prevent yourself from growing stagnant.

The most challenging aspect is often deciding to plunge into unfamiliar territory. Yet you always need to ask yourself - what's the worst possible outcome?

Binocular Effect

The dismissal from my first employment was a devastating experience. It left me in a state of despair, questioning why I had to endure this pain. I was at a loss, wondering what transgressions I had committed for it to happen. The same feelings of despair ensued when my venture failed, and my dreams seemed to crumble, or when I felt a deep sense of betrayal from a trusted business associate.

These occurrences were emotionally shattering at the time. However, I realised two crucial factors: first, they were beyond my control, and second, they played a significant role in shaping my current position.

I acknowledge that if I had not been terminated from that job, I might not have been in the position I am in today. Perhaps this was because one path was obstructed, forcing me to explore other avenues. This journey led me to my current position, which I now understand was crucial.

Let's consider binoculars as an analogy. When used correctly, we can see distant objects with greater clarity. However, when used in reverse, as children often do, objects appear even more distant than they are. At times, this perspective is precisely what is needed in life.

Specifically, when examining fragments of your life up close, you will likely encounter numerous setbacks, traumas, and periods of sadness. However, when you step back and view a more significant portion of your life, you will find that each phase is consistently better than the last.

By adopting this perspective, you can alleviate stress. Focusing on life's details can be stressful, whereas taking a broader view tends to be less so. Therefore, one method to reduce stress and learn to accept that you are not in control of everything is to adopt a broader perspective, akin to using binoculars in reverse. I genuinely believe that my hardships eventually brought me joy because I accepted the many things beyond my control. And for every one of those times, I continue to tell myself and believe that the lessons learned will benefit me in the future. And they have.

Everything Happens for a Reason

The fact is that life seldom follows the blueprint we lay out for it in our youth. Perhaps you have a plan, put in the effort, stay focused, and believe that in doing so, you will reach your goals. As a meticulous planner, you likely appreciate routine and stability. And it would be great if life worked that way, to know what the future holds and for it to remain on the script we have in our head.

Often, life deviates from our expectations. You might find yourself jobless, divorced, or diagnosed with an illness. It's challenging to come to terms with unforeseen and undesirable obstacles.

Take a moment to examine your feelings when life presents you with unexpected difficulties or when things seem chaotic. These emotions likely result from criticising and holding yourself accountable for circumstances beyond your control.

Not every incident is your fault. Of course, you are at fault sometimes, and owning up is crucial when you genuinely make a mistake. But I'm referring to all the unpredictable events that life throws your way that leave you disoriented because they don't align with your expectations or desires.

No matter how much effort you put in, how competent you are, or what actions you take, there are some matters you don't have any control over. Attempting to control all situations and striving for a flawless life is exhausting and impractical.

It's an immense load to bear—the expectation that you can keep everything in order, never blunder, always make the right decisions and prevent catastrophes. Assuming responsibility for controlling and rectifying everything is unrealistic and unnecessary. Accepting that life is erratic and occasionally uncontrollable enables progress.

Your effort will not be banked if you remain entangled in the pain and struggle of attempting to manage, mend, and alter things beyond your control. Rather than banking your effort, you are utilising all of it to change the current situation and yield the desired results. Perfection is not possible.

Maintaining a firm grip on your desires and expectations is an option, or you can choose to let go of them, accepting the current reality. Recognising what's beyond your control does not imply you're trapped or destined for unhappiness. While you cannot alter circumstances or people, you control your thoughts, emotions, and actions.

Understanding that many aspects are beyond your grasp isn't about surrendering or capitulating. It's not a sign of weakness or passivity, nor does it mean others triumph while you fail. It's simply distinguishing between illusion and truth, enabling you to focus your energy on what's within your control.

The first step is acknowledging your present circumstances. It would be best to reassure yourself that every event in life has a purpose. Any hardship you're experiencing is not coincidental. Instead, view it as a chance for a fresh start. You have the potential for significant accomplishments, but it requires accepting your past and growing from it. If you manage to do this, you can anticipate positive changes.

CHAPTER THREE

BELIEF IN THE EFFORT BANK

AT THE HEART OF EVERY endeavour, belief is the cornerstone upon which all efforts are built. This chapter delves into the profound role that belief plays within the framework of Effort Bank, a concept that champions investing effort with the assurance of future rewards. However, this assurance is not merely a matter of faith; it's a conviction rooted in the understanding that our efforts are never in vain, provided we genuinely believe in their potential.

Belief, in the context of the Effort Bank, transcends the conventional. It's an unwavering trust in the process, a steadfast confidence that our deposits of hard work and dedication will yield dividends of success. This chapter explores how belief is not just about expecting positive outcomes but preparing oneself for the journey of highs and lows with a resilient mindset. The essence of belief here is twofold: believing in the existence and efficacy of the Effort Bank and, more importantly, believing in oneself.

The journey through the Effort Bank is akin to navigating the complex terrains of life where victories and setbacks are part of the landscape. Belief acts as the compass that guides us through these terrains, ensuring that our efforts are purposeful and our spirits undeterred. It's about embracing the certainty that while success may not be immediate, the persistence of belief coupled with effort inevitably leads to achievement.

Learning Gratitude

Gratitude is a transformative force in personal development, a theme that underscores its power in shaping our perspectives and life experiences. Cultivating gratitude involves recognising and appreciating the value in every moment and aspect of our lives, from the monumental achievements to the subtle, often overlooked everyday blessings. This practice is not merely about acknowledging what we have; it's about altering our relationship with our circumstances, fostering a mindset that emphasises abundance over scarcity and possibilities over limitations.

The journey to ingratitude begins with small, intentional steps. Keeping a gratitude journal, which records daily gratitude, can significantly enhance our awareness and appreciation of life's gifts. This habit encourages us to look beyond our challenges and frustrations, focusing instead on what enriches our lives. Additionally, expressing gratitude to others strengthens our relationships and amplifies our sense of well-being and connectedness.

Gratitude is also profoundly linked to resilience. By valuing what we have, we build a buffer against adversity, enabling us to navigate life's inevitable ups and downs with grace and strength. It shifts our focus from what we lack to the resources and strengths we possess, fostering a sense of sufficiency that can propel us through challenging times.

With its power to transform our perspective and enrich our life experience, gratitude naturally segues into the realm of attitude. Cultivating a deep appreciation for what we have can foster an attitude poised for resilience, positivity, and proactive engagement with the world.

Attitude

Attitude is the lens through which we view the world, interpret our experiences, and interact with others. It encompasses our willingness to learn, adapt, collaborate, and push through challenges. A positive attitude is often synonymous with a growth mindset—a belief in the possibility of improvement through effort and learning. In contrast, skills are specific abilities or expertise that can be acquired and measured.

In the professional sphere, attitude significantly outweighs skills, marking a definitive stance on what truly matters in shaping an individual's success. Skills are undoubtedly advantageous, but attitude is the cornerstone of true potential. Envisioning this dynamic through a unique framework, imagine an A-Team quadrant model, a concept I teach during one of my training sessions, which helps illustrate the varied interplays between attitude and skills.

A. **Having both Attitude and Skills:** This group has the right attitude and required skills. In any professional capacity, this is the most desired group.

B. **Skills without Attitude:** This category represents individuals with the necessary skills but lack the right attitude. While their expertise may be undeniable, their growth and contribution to a team are limited by their inability to adapt, collaborate effectively, or embrace challenges. Such individuals may excel in roles that require little change or interaction but struggle in environments that demand constant innovation and teamwork.

C. **Attitude without Skills:** Individuals with a robust and positive attitude but lacking specific skills are often considered the most desirable by visionary leaders. Their rationale is straightforward: skills can be taught, but attitude is ingrained. People with the right attitude are seen as blank slates with unlimited potential. They possess the adaptability, eagerness to learn, and resilience that make them invaluable in a dynamic, fast-paced work environment.

D. **Lacking Both Skills and Attitude:** Unsurprisingly, individuals lacking skills and the right attitude are considered the least desirable. Without either foundation, their ability to contribute to or grow within an organisation is significantly hampered.

If a CEO is faced with the decision of choosing between candidates A and D for a job or task, the choice is clear - A will be selected over D. However, when it comes to deciding between candidates B and C, C will be preferred over B due to the importance of attitude. Preferring attitude over skills is not merely a matter of philosophy; it's a strategic choice rooted in the realities of the modern workplace.

Preferring attitude over skills is not merely a matter of philosophy; it's a strategic choice rooted in the realities of the modern workplace.

Adaptability: Adapting is paramount in an era of rapid technological advancements and constant change. Individuals with the right attitude embrace change, seek out learning opportunities, and are more likely to thrive in uncertain environments.

Collaboration: A positive attitude fosters teamwork and collaboration. Individuals who are open, willing to share ideas, and support their colleagues contribute to a positive work culture that drives collective success.

Innovation: Creativity and innovation require a mindset that sees beyond the status quo. A positive attitude encourages curiosity and a willingness to experiment and take calculated risks.

Leadership Potential: Those with the right attitude naturally inspire others. They embody the qualities of resilience, optimism, and a commitment to growth that are essential for effective leadership.

Recognising the supremacy of attitude does not diminish the value of skills but rather repositions them within a broader context of personal and professional development. The challenge for individuals and organisations is to nurture the right attitudes while facilitating skill development. This involves creating learning cultures, offering growth opportunities, and recognising and rewarding attitudes that contribute to collective success.

In conclusion, the 'A-Team quadrant' concept emphasises that having the right attitude is paramount. The importance of attitude over skills highlights a fundamental principle for achieving personal fulfilment and organisational success. It underscores the belief that while skills are crucial, the right attitude is the catalyst that unlocks potential, drives growth, and fosters innovation. As we navigate the complexities of the modern world, this perspective serves as a guiding light for individuals seeking to maximise their impact and organisations aiming to cultivate environments where talent and potential can flourish.

It's Not Luck, It's Effort Bank

The "Effort Bank" notion challenges the common misconception that success is a matter of luck. Instead, it posits that success is the cumulative result of consistent effort, dedication, and perseverance. Every action we take, every hour we dedicate to our goals, and every setback we overcome contributes to our "Effort Bank," a symbolic repository of our invested energy and persistence.

This perspective emphasises the importance of hard work, discipline, and a proactive stance toward achieving our objectives. It suggests that while luck may play a role in success, our efforts lay the groundwork for opportunities to arise and for us to capitalise on them. The "Effort Bank" concept encourages us to view each effort, no matter how small, as a valuable deposit into our future success.

Embracing this mindset fosters a sense of agency and responsibility for our outcomes. It motivates us to engage actively in our pursuits, understanding that our investments of time and energy are crucial to realising our ambitions. Moreover, it cultivates patience and resilience, as we recognise that the benefits of our efforts may not be immediate but are accumulating, preparing us for future success.

Addressing the concept of luck is crucial in dispelling a common misconception that often hinders personal accountability and growth. The notion of being a perpetual victim, a mindset I encountered at a training session years ago inspired by the book "SUMO (Shut Up, Move On)," needs to be challenged. This perspective, where one views oneself as a victim of circumstance, effectively blocks the path to taking responsibility for one's actions and outcomes.

The idea that success or failure is merely a matter of luck is a detrimental belief. It leads to a mindset where external forces, rather than personal effort and choices, are blamed for one's situation. This belief system fosters a sense of helplessness and resentment towards others perceived as more 'fortunate.' However, as discussed in various professional circles, the true essence of luck is not a whimsical favour bestowed by the universe. Instead, it is an acronym for 'Labour Under Correct Knowledge.' This interpretation of luck underscores the importance of acquiring accurate knowledge and diligently applying oneself through informed effort.

Success, therefore, is not a lottery of birthright, language, or skin colour; it is the result of directed hard work and the application of knowledge. By redefining luck, we shift the focus from external attributions to internal action, encouraging individuals to take charge of their destiny through informed and persistent effort.

The Power of Positive Thinking

The power of positive thinking is not just an optimistic attitude towards life but a strategic approach to problem-solving and goal achievement. This mindset focuses on solutions, opportunities, and constructive outcomes rather than dwelling on obstacles, problems, and pessimistic predictions. Positive thinking is about expecting the best and actively making the best happen through positive actions, affirmations, and emotional resilience.

Adopting a positive mindset increases our ability to cope with stress, challenges, and adversity. It enhances creativity, boosts energy, and improves overall health. Moreover, it attracts positive outcomes and opportunities, as we are more likely to take actions that align with our positive expectations and to recognise and seize opportunities when they arise.

We can practice visualisation techniques, affirmations, and mindfulness to harness the power of positive thinking. These practices help us reframe our thoughts, focus on positive outcomes, and maintain an optimistic outlook despite difficulties. Doing so improves our mental and emotional well-being and sets the stage for achieving our personal and professional goals.

Again, this is what we do in our training events when I present the concept of the Effort Bank. I start by asking the participants: if you win, how do you celebrate? Typically, they respond that they celebrate by jumping up and down, expressing joy. Then, I ask if you lose, what do you do? Before being introduced to the Effort Bank concept, they often say they feel sad, cry, or seek solitude. However, their perspective shifted after I explained the Effort Bank to them and asked again how they would celebrate a win or handle a loss.

The response remains the same for victories: jumping, celebrating, and happiness. But interestingly, their approach to handling defeat changes; they now say they would celebrate losses in the same manner as they do wins because they are now aware that their efforts are not wasted, and it doesn't matter if they don't get paid now; they will get paid later on.

At this point, I play music in the hall, encouraging everyone to celebrate. "Let's celebrate our failures just like this," I say, enabling them to jump and dance. This usually leaves some participants sceptical or confused, wondering if it's sane to celebrate failures as if they were victories. But this is the essence of positive thinking—applying a positive spin to everything in life because dwelling in sadness won't change the outcome.

Then, we delve into the topic of luck. Some might argue that luck is a divine gift and that God preordains success or failure. They believe that if they're unlucky, divine favour isn't on their side, and the only recourse is to pray for better fortune next time.

While prayer and drawing closer to one's faith are essential, regardless of religious beliefs, it's crucial to understand that luck, as we perceive it, is not a creation of the divine. I argue that God, in His omniscience, created the universe and its governing laws—physics, chemistry, nature—and then allowed them to operate independently.

He doesn't interfere daily, choosing who succeeds or fails based on favouritism. Our success is not about being chosen by God for luck; it's about the choices we make and the efforts we put into our pursuits.

For instance, if someone were to sit at home, praying to become wealthy without effort, it's improbable that their prayers would be answered.

Yes, God has the power to do anything, but the principle of non-interference means that our outcomes are determined mainly by our actions, not by waiting for divine intervention. This narrative emphasises the power of effort over luck and the importance of proactive engagement in shaping our destinies.

In summary, this chapter points out the focal role of belief in the concept of the effort bank, advocating that success is derived from persistent effort rather than luck. It stresses the importance of viewing efforts as valuable investments stored in the Effort Bank for future rewards, fostering a mindset of resilience and positivity towards life's challenges.

By debunking the myth of luck as a determinant of success and highlighting the significance of effort and knowledge, the chapter encourages a shift towards a proactive approach to achieving goals.

It also introduces psychological concepts like acceptance, gratitude, and the superiority of attitude over skills. It offers a comprehensive strategy for personal and professional growth through continuous effort and belief in the power of the Effort Bank.

CHAPTER FOUR

POSITIVE SIDE OF FAILURE

OFTEN FEARED AND AVOIDED, failure is an inevitable part of the human experience. Yet, it holds immense potential for personal and professional growth. This chapter delves into the transformative power of failure, highlighting how setbacks can lead to significant opportunities, provided we view them holistically. It challenges the traditional narrative of failure as a negative outcome, proposing that failure is a critical step toward success.

In the following pages, I seek to illuminate the transformative power in the heart of failure. It posits that setbacks, rather than signalling the end of a journey, can pave the way for new, unforeseen opportunities. By adopting a holistic perspective that embraces successes and failures as integral components of progress, we can uncover the latent potential that failure holds for personal and professional development.

Traditionally, failure is cast negatively as a stark deviation from the path to success. This view reinforces a fear-based approach to challenges, where avoiding failure becomes a driving force, often at the expense of innovation, learning, and growth. This chapter challenges such a narrative by repositioning failure as an essential stepping stone rather than a detour on the road to achievement.

Embracing failure involves a profound shift in perspective. It requires seeing beyond the immediate disappointment and recognising the seeds of opportunity that failure sows. This perspective doesn't trivialise the pain and frustration that often accompany setbacks but acknowledges them as part of a more extensive, more complex process of growth and discovery.

Through this lens, failure is redefined as a powerful agent of change, capable of fostering resilience, inspiring creativity, and teaching invaluable lessons that success alone could never impart. By understanding and embracing the positive aspects of failure, we unlock the potential to transform our most challenging moments into our most significant opportunities for learning and growth.

Failure Leads to Opportunity

Often seen as a setback, failure holds the potential for opportunity and growth. It serves as a rigorous teacher, providing lessons that success cannot. Each failure carves out a path for introspection, urging us to question our methods, assumptions, and strategies.

This process of self-examination opens doors to innovative thinking and exploring paths less travelled. The stories of countless successful entrepreneurs, scientists, and artists echo this sentiment, where their most significant breakthroughs were preceded by periods of profound failure. Embracing failure as an opportunity requires a paradigm shift in our perception, seeing it not as a deterrent but as a catalyst for exploration and reinvention.

My friends perceive me as successful, envisioning a life filled with travel, awards, lifestyle, luxury, investments, and properties. They believe I've unlocked a secret formula to consistently choose winning paths over losing ones. From their perspective, I never fail. This superficial view, however, misses the crucial detail that my journey has been punctuated with failures—sometimes two, sometimes ten, and at times even more before achieving success. The common misconception is that a rational person would surrender after repeated failures, interpreting these setbacks as signs from the divine that success is not destined. Yet, I keep it up, driven by the belief in depositing efforts into the 'Effort Bank,' leading to eventual success that overshadows the numerous attempts unseen by others. This persistence is often mistakenly attributed to luck because it's human nature to categorise unexplained phenomena into understandable constructs.

The cycle I often experience goes fail, fail, then win. Sometimes, there are only two failures before I win. Other times, failure repeats itself ten, twenty, or more times. However, the essence lies in perseverance; I persist where many would advise quitting. Logically, after numerous attempts and failures, one might conclude it's wise to cease efforts. Some may interpret persistent failure as a signal that success is not predestined. Yet, this perspective overlooks the crucial role of personal effort and determination.

I don't subscribe to the idea of predestined failure; instead, I believe in the principle of the "effort bank." Regardless of its immediate outcome, each attempt is an investment in this bank. The belief that every effort contributes to eventual success fuels my resilience, pushing me beyond apparent logic and societal expectations of when to give up.

Upon my 11th, 12th, or even 15th attempt, when I finally succeeded, my friends only saw the triumph, not the preceding 14 attempts. They exclaim, "Oh, he's done something remarkable. He's so lucky!" attributing my success to luck. This reaction stems from a lack of understanding of the Effort Bank concept.

The human brain naturally seeks explanations for the inexplicable, preferring to categorise and label phenomena to make sense of them. It wonders why one person achieves success seemingly effortlessly while others do not and conjures reasons ranging from divine will to luck, nationality, appearance, or language. These rationalisations are our way of making sense of the world, yet they often miss the mark.

Success hinges not on external factors but on consistent investment in the Effort Bank. While we may conjure various explanations to satisfy our need for understanding, the truth often lies in effort banking. Persistence proves fruitful when you consistently deposit effort into your pursuits.

View Negatives Holistically

Adopting a holistic perspective towards adverse outcomes is imperative to harness the full potential of failure. This involves understanding the interconnectedness of our experiences and recognising that setbacks are an integral part of the journey to success. A holistic view allows us to appreciate the value in every experience, encouraging resilience and adaptability. It teaches us to balance our emotional responses to failure, preventing despair and fostering a constructive mindset that seeks lessons and avenues for growth in every setback.

Setbacks are not merely hurdles to be overcome but essential components of the learning process. They provide valuable lessons, insights, and opportunities for self-reflection and growth. Each failure teaches resilience, encourages innovation, and fosters adaptability—indispensable qualities for long-term success.

The interconnectedness of our experiences means that every action, decision, and outcome is linked. A setback in one area can lead to an opportunity in another, often in ways that are not immediately apparent. This interconnectedness encourages a holistic view of success, which values the journey as much as the destination.

Recognising setbacks as integral to success also involves embracing a growth mindset. Instead of a fixed mindset, this mindset believes in the potential for development and improvement through effort and learning from failures. It's the belief that abilities like resilience can be developed through dedication and hard work. Resilience is not about avoiding failure but knowing how to deal with it effectively, learning from it, and moving forward with increased strength and wisdom. It involves recognising that setbacks are not a reflection of one's worth but rather an opportunity for growth and learning.

Balancing Our Emotional Responses to Failure

Balancing our emotional responses to failure is crucial for maintaining mental well-being and fostering personal growth. Failure, by its nature, can elicit strong emotions such as disappointment, frustration, and sadness. While it's natural and healthy to experience these emotions, managing them effectively is equally important to prevent them from becoming overwhelming or debilitating.

The first step in balancing emotional responses is acknowledging and accepting your feelings. Denying or suppressing emotions can lead to increased stress and anxiety. Instead, permit yourself to feel disappointed or upset, but limit how long you will allow these feelings to dominate your thoughts. This practice helps in recognising emotions without letting them control your actions.

Practising self-compassion is another vital aspect of managing emotional responses to failure. Be kind to yourself and recognise that failure is a universal experience. Instead of self-criticism, remind yourself that every individual face setbacks and that they do not define your worth or capabilities.

Reframing your perspective on failure can also help balance emotional responses. View failures as learning opportunities or stepping stones to success. This mindset shift can transform negative emotions into motivation and curiosity, making it easier to bounce back and move forward.

Establishing a support system is essential for emotional balance. Sharing your experiences with trusted friends, family, or mentors can provide comfort, reassurance, and different perspectives. Simply verbalising your feelings and receiving empathy can significantly reduce the emotional weight of failure.

Engaging in activities that promote emotional regulation, such as mindfulness, meditation, or physical exercise, can also be beneficial. These practices can help calm the mind, reduce stress, and improve your ability to manage emotions constructively.

Finally, setting realistic goals and expectations is critical to minimising the emotional impact of setbacks. While ambition is important, unrealistic expectations can lead to frequent disappointments. By setting achievable goals and celebrating small successes, you can maintain a positive outlook and resilience in the face of challenges.

Hold Onto Your Vision

In the face of failure, holding onto your vision becomes crucial. This vision is a lighthouse guiding us through the stormy seas of doubt and setbacks. It provides a sense of purpose and direction, anchoring us to our goals despite the tumultuous journey.

The resolve to cling to this vision differentiates the successful from the rest, even when the odds are stacked against us. The unwavering belief in our dreams and capabilities propels us forward, turning apparent failures into stepping stones towards our ultimate objectives.

The power of a clear, compelling vision lies in its ability to offer perspective. When faced with failure, it's easy to become ensnared in the immediacy of disappointment and lose sight of the bigger picture. However, a well-defined vision helps us rise above the momentary setbacks, reminding us of the larger purpose and the reasons we embarked on this journey in the first place. It reorients our focus from what we've lost to what is still waiting to be achieved.

Moreover, holding onto our vision fosters resilience. It's a testament to our capacity to endure, adapt, and persevere. This resolve, the determination to keep our eyes on the prize, even when beset by challenges, distinguishes the truly successful. It's about understanding that the path to achievement is seldom straight but is often a mosaic of trials, errors, and lessons learned. Each failure, viewed through the lens of our vision, becomes a lesson rather than a setback, a necessary step in the refinement of our strategies and ourselves.

Our vision also serves as a source of motivation and inspiration. In moments of doubt, it reminds us of our passion and why and reignites the spark to push forward. This unwavering belief in our dreams and ourselves is a powerful force, propelling us towards our goals with renewed vigour and determination. It's the fuel that keeps us moving forward, turning apparent obstacles into opportunities for growth and learning.

Ultimately, holding onto our vision in the face of failure is about more than perseverance; it's about transformation. It challenges us to grow, expand our capabilities, and emerge more assertive, skilled, and determined. It teaches us that true success is not just about reaching our destination but also about our journey, the challenges we overcome, and the person we become.

Our vision is our north star, guiding us through uncertainty, inspiring us to rise after each fall, and leading us towards realising our deepest aspirations. It reminds us that, regardless of our obstacles, our dreams remain within reach, urging us to press on, adapt, and transform failures into the foundations of our future successes.

In conclusion, the positive side of failure is multifaceted, offering opportunities for growth, a deeper understanding of our journey, refinement of our efforts, and a test of our commitment to our vision.

By embracing failure, viewing it holistically, polishing our efforts, and holding onto our vision, we can navigate the complexities of our accomplishments with resilience and optimism. Thus, failure becomes an inevitable part of our journey and an asset in our quest for success.

CHAPTER FIVE

MANAGE FEAR

FEAR OFTEN STEMS FROM feeling unprepared or lacking the necessary skills (keys) to achieve our goals. By framing our journey using the Effort Bank concept, we can see fear not as an insurmountable barrier but as an indication of which skills or efforts we still need to acquire or enhance. The Effort Bank encourages a shift in focus from immediate results to consistent effort and skill development. This perspective can significantly reduce anxiety related to success or failure by emphasising that value lies in the effort and learning, not just the outcome.

By visualising each effort and new skill as a deposit into the Effort Bank, we can appreciate incremental progress even when immediate results are not visible. This gradual accumulation of skills and efforts helps build confidence, reducing fear as we recognise our growing ability to tackle challenges. The concept teaches patience and trust by illustrating that rewards may require extensive effort and multiple skills to unlock. This understanding can alleviate the fear of failure by framing setbacks as part of the journey towards accumulating the necessary keys for success.

Action is an Antidote to Fear. The call to action inherent in the Effort Bank model is to continuously act, learn, and adapt. It reassures us that every action, whether it leads to success or provides experience, is valuable. This proactive approach can diminish fear by reinforcing that action and engagement are within our control, even when outcomes are not.

Take Massive Action

In my journey towards achieving greatness, I've learned that acting is the most effective antidote to fear. It's not just about being brave; it's about moving forward even when every fibre of your being wants to retreat. This realisation didn't come quickly to me, but through experiences and deliberate choices, I've found ways to push through the fear and step into action.

Most recently, one of the pivotal moments for me was deciding to pursue my passion despite the overwhelming fear of failure—the thought of venturing into unknown territory, where the possibility of failing loomed large, was paralysing. However, I realised that fear of failure was a constant companion on the path to success.

I remembered reading about successful entrepreneurs who embraced failure as an essential part of their journey. People like Steve Jobs and Elon Musk faced numerous setbacks but never let fear dictate their actions. Inspired by their resilience, I chose to leap, understanding that failure was not the opposite of success but a stepping stone towards it.

Another significant challenge I faced was public speaking. The mere thought of standing in front of a crowd was enough to send shivers down my spine. However, I knew that to spread my message and make an enormous impact, I had to conquer this fear. Drawing inspiration from renowned speakers like Brené Brown and Tony Robbins, who spoke candidly about their initial fears and how they overcame them, I decided to take small steps. I started by talking to small groups, gradually increasing the audience size. Each time, I focused not on what could go wrong but on the message, I wanted to convey. This shift in perspective from fear to purpose was transformative.

Choosing to be vulnerable was perhaps the most challenging action I took. Sharing my struggles, doubts, and failures felt like standing naked in front of a crowd. Yet, I remembered reading about the power of vulnerability in Brené Brown's work. She argued that vulnerability is not a weakness but a profound strength. Encouraged by her research, I began to share my journey, warts and all. The response was astonishing. Not only did it help others feel less alone in their struggles, but it also deepened my connections and made my work more impactful.

Research in psychology supports the approach of taking action over succumbing to fear. Studies show that action-oriented individuals exhibit higher resilience and are more likely to achieve their goals. They use fear as a signal, not a deterrent. This aligns with the concept of "feel the fear and do it anyway," Susan Jeffers popularised. It's about recognising fear as a natural response to the unknown but not allowing it to impede progress.

Taking action in the face of fear has been a transformative experience for me. Each step has been a victory over the paralysing grip of fear, no matter how small. It's a journey that requires patience, resilience, and the willingness to be vulnerable. But the rewards—personal growth, success, and the ability to impact others—are immeasurably worth it. I say to anyone at the crossroads of action and fear: choose action. It's the path to discovering your true potential and achieving greatness.

Learning is on the Other Side of Fear

I've always believed that the accurate measure of courage isn't the absence of fear but rather the mastery over it. The journey to discovering one's true potential is fraught with uncertainties, challenges, and considerable fear. However, it is in navigating these very hurdles that we uncover lessons invaluable to our personal and professional growth.

The first step in overcoming fear is to confront it head-on. Fear, in its essence, is a protective mechanism designed to alert us to potential dangers. Yet, it often becomes a barrier to our growth, holding us back from pursuing opportunities beyond our comfort zones. I learned this lesson during a pivotal moment in my career when I was faced with a choice: continue the familiar path or venture into the unknown, where the possibility of failure loomed large. The fear of the unknown was palpable, but the realisation that staying stagnant was a greater risk to my growth propelled me forward.

Embracing vulnerability is perhaps one of the most challenging aspects of confronting fear. Being vulnerable is acknowledging our fears, doubts, and insecurities, exposing ourselves to potential criticism and failure. However, it is precisely through this exposure that we find strength and resilience. Vulnerability allows us to connect with others more deeply, fostering relationships built on trust and mutual understanding. It also opens the door to feedback, which is sometimes difficult to accept but is essential for personal and professional development.

The journey through fear taught me several invaluable lessons. The first is the importance of resilience. Each time we face our fears and emerge on the other side, we build a little more resilience, equipping us with the strength to tackle future challenges. The second lesson is the power of adaptability. By stepping out of our comfort zones, we learn to adapt to new situations, an increasingly important skill in today's ever-changing world.

The most significant lesson, however, is the realisation that growth and comfort cannot coexist. Proper growth requires us to push beyond the boundaries of what feels safe, to challenge ourselves, and to take risks. In the moments when we feel most uncertain, we have the opportunity to learn the most about ourselves and redefine what we can achieve.

Reflecting on my journey, I am reminded that the lessons learned on the other side of fear shape us into who we are meant to become. They teach us about our strengths, weaknesses, and, most importantly, our capacity for change. So, to those standing on the precipice of decision, feeling the weight of fear holding you back, I encourage you to take that leap. The path may not be easy, but the lessons you'll learn, the growth you'll experience, and the person you'll become will be worth every step of the journey.

From Childhood Courage to Adult Fear

Nearly all accidents can be prevented, especially in the crucial moment just before they occur. If, at that last second, one keeps their eyes open and refrains from resigning to fate with thoughts of doom, there's a possibility of manoeuvre or avoiding the accident altogether.

Often, the overwhelming sense of fear inhibits action, making the removal of fear an essential aspect of my training. I frequently reference a video I saw years ago, which contrasts the fearless actions of our childhood—climbing trees and walls, activities now deemed risky—with our adult apprehensions. As children, we engaged in these activities without fear, rarely resulting in more than a broken leg and, indeed, not death. The video showcases a child's boundless imagination, visualising themselves as superheroes like Superman or Spider-Man, believing in their ability to conquer the world without limitations.

However, as we grow, societal norms and input from parents, teachers, and peers instil a sense of doubt and fear about our capabilities. They caution us about the harsh realities of life, dampening our dreams with scepticism. This negativity, reinforced by personal setbacks such as job rejections or dismissals, cements a belief in the difficulties of real life, validating the warnings of our elders. This fear, then, becomes a barrier to achieving our dreams. The video emphasises that maintaining the fearlessness of childhood into adulthood could lead to extraordinary accomplishments. Many of the most successful individuals have managed to preserve this inner child's fearlessness, demonstrating the profound impact of overcoming fear.

The concept of the Effort Bank plays a crucial role in mitigating fear. In my travels and interactions across sixty countries, I've observed that fear of failure significantly hinders success. Despite their best intentions, parents often discourage their children from pursuing ambitious dreams to protect them from potential disappointment. This protective instinct, though well-meaning, can inadvertently stifle a child's potential. It is essential to understand that fear, especially the fear instilled in us from a young age, can be overcome through support, encouragement, and the strategic use of the Effort Bank to build resilience and pursue success fearlessly.

Never Give Up

Mental toughness and the unwavering resolve to never give up have been cornerstones of my journey, especially when faced with adversity. This resilience has been more than just a trait; it's a cultivated skill deeply integrated into the ethos of the Effort Bank concept that I developed and adhere to. The principle of depositing effort, regardless of immediate acknowledgement or reward, has guided me through times of uncertainty and challenge.

Mental toughness, for me, isn't just about enduring hard times; it's about seeing these moments as opportunities for growth and learning. It's the understanding that every challenge, every rejection, and every failure is a deposit into my Effort Bank, accumulating a wealth of experience and resilience that will pay dividends in the future. This perspective has allowed me to transform potential setbacks into lessons and stepping stones towards my goals.

My journey has been filled with moments that tested my mental toughness and resolve, from embarking on ventures without contacts or knowledge of the local language to facing personal and professional crises that could have easily broken my spirit. Yet, during these times, the Effort Bank concept proved most valuable. Each challenge was an investment, each struggle a deposit, enriching my reservoir of strength and determination.

The Grind is Good

In earlier chapters, I've highlighted the significance of hard work and consistently emphasised the value of embracing challenges and the lessons they offer. I recall a particular incident where one of the employees was seen hurriedly moving back and forth in a corridor. When inquired about her behaviour, she was overheard repeatedly muttering, "The grind is good, the grind is good." Upon further questioning, she explained that despite facing difficulties that day, she remembered my assertion that enduring such hardships is beneficial. She believed that overcoming these challenges was making her stronger.

Indeed, the concepts of perseverance and mental fortitude enhance one's strength. Napoleon Hill, in his work "Think and Grow Rich," even suggested that poverty is akin to mental illness—a bold statement, undoubtedly. This notion does not simplify poverty but highlights the profound impact of mental resilience. Being mentally robust enables one to navigate through challenges effectively.

Reflecting on my experiences, there was a time when unforeseen obstacles in projects or imminent deadlines would lead to panic and a sense of helplessness among my team and me. Such situations, seemingly inevitable in every project, used to overwhelm us, leaving us mentally defeated.

However, my current approach in similar circumstances is markedly different. Despite facing disruptions, I remain composed and capable of addressing the issue without allowing it to undermine my resolve. This change does not stem from a lack of concern for the projects but rather from enhanced mental resilience. This grit will enable me to remain calm and collected amidst challenges and significantly contribute to my ability to manage situations more effectively.

Diamonds Vs. Coal

In my training, I often draw parallels between diamonds and coal to illustrate a powerful concept. Both diamonds and coal are composed of carbon, sharing the same chemical makeup. Under a microscope, their intrinsic similarities are undeniable. Yet, the value we ascribe to each could not be more different. This distinction lies not in their composition but in the transformative journey from coal to diamond—a process defined by extreme heat and pressure, conditions that are difficult to fathom. This physical and symbolic transformation represents potential, transformation, and the value of enduring challenges.

We liken this conversion to the concept of an "Effort Bank." As coal endures these severe conditions, it's depositing pain and struggle into an Effort Bank without immediate signs of change or victory. Yet, enduring and persevering through adversity culminates in a remarkable transformation. Suddenly, what was once coal emerges as a diamond, now prized and valued, no longer dismissed or overlooked. This transition from being inconsequential to becoming an integral part of a crown symbolises the profound impact of perseverance and resilience. It serves as a reminder that the challenges and pressures we face are not merely obstacles but opportunities for growth and transformation, leading us from the ordinary to the extraordinary.

Let us examine the application of Diamond Vs. Coal analogy to the Effort Bank. As coal transforms into a diamond through extreme conditions, individuals can grow and develop through challenges. The Effort Bank concept mirrors this process, suggesting that the efforts and struggles we deposit over time contribute to our eventual success and transformation. Each challenge faced is like the heat and pressure applied to coal, a necessary part of the journey toward becoming our best selves.

Value of Persistence. The journey from coal to diamond underscores the importance of persistence. Just as coal does not become a diamond overnight, meaningful personal growth and achievement result from sustained effort and resilience. Depositing into the Effort Bank means embracing each failure, setback, or challenge as an opportunity to grow, learn, and edge closer to our goals.

Recognising Potential. The analogy also highlights the potential within everyone, regardless of their current state or circumstances. Just as every piece of coal can become a diamond, every person can achieve greatness through continuous effort, learning, and adaptation.

The Role of Environment. Just as the transformation of coal into a diamond requires a specific environment of heat and pressure, our environments often catalyse personal growth and the pressures we face. This suggests that seeking out and embracing challenging situations can be a deliberate strategy for growth, pushing us to deposit more into our Effort Bank and accelerate our transformation.

The "diamonds and coal" analogy is a powerful reminder of the transformative power of adversity and effort. It encourages us to view our struggles not as insurmountable obstacles but as necessary steps in our personal development journey. By embracing the concept of the Effort Bank, we acknowledge that every effort, challenge, and failure overcome is a deposit toward becoming our most resilient, capable, and valuable selves—our version of a diamond.

Self-motivation

Self-motivation plays a crucial role in the Effort Bank as it serves as the driving force behind consistent and persistent effort. In the context of Effort Bank, self-motivation is the internal engine that propels individuals to invest their energy and resources into their goals, even in the face of challenges and setbacks. When individuals are self-motivated, they are more likely to maintain a positive attitude, stay focused on their objectives, and persevere through difficulties.

This inner drive encourages them to continue depositing efforts into the Effort Bank, knowing their dedication will eventually lead to rewards. Without self-motivation, individuals may struggle to sustain their commitment to their goals, making it difficult to accumulate the necessary efforts in the effort bank. Therefore, cultivating and harnessing self-motivation is essential for effectively utilising the Effort Bank concept to achieve long-term success and personal growth.

One aspect of self-motivation is the ability to set clear and achievable goals. Individuals define specific objectives by providing a roadmap for progress and a sense of purpose. These goals serve as beacons, guiding actions and decisions towards desired outcomes. Moreover, self-motivation involves maintaining a positive mindset despite setbacks or obstacles encountered along the way. It entails cultivating resilience and perseverance, viewing challenges as opportunities for growth rather than deterrents to success.

Furthermore, self-motivation encompasses self-discipline and accountability. It involves taking ownership of one's actions and commitments, staying focused on priorities, and adhering to deadlines. This sense of discipline ensures that individuals remain steadfast in their pursuit of excellence, even when faced with distractions or temptations.

Additionally, self-motivation fosters a sense of intrinsic satisfaction and fulfilment derived from pursuing goals. It is about finding joy and meaning in the journey rather than solely focusing on the result. By embracing this perspective, individuals can sustain their motivation over the long term, even when faced with challenges or setbacks.

The Ripple Effect of Self-Motivation

I used to believe that achieving significant feats required monumental efforts akin to those of iconic leaders and philanthropists. However, a simple yet profound anecdote reshaped my perspective, illuminating the essence of self-motivation through consistent action. The story unfolds with a man walking along a stormy beach, witnessing the relentless force of the ocean casting numerous fish onto the shore. Undeterred by the overwhelming odds, he begins the arduous task of returning each fish to the water, one by one.

When questioned about the seemingly futile effort, he calmly explains that while he cannot save them all at once, every fish returned to the water makes a tangible difference. This narrative struck a chord with me, prompting reflection on my journey of traversing the globe, conducting training sessions, and engaging with diverse individuals. Along the way, I've encountered countless tales of personal triumph, each a testament to the transformative power of self-motivation.

One such encounter unfolded in Slovenia, a European country, where a woman approached me after a training session to share her inspiring journey. She revealed that spurred by the motivation instilled during our interaction, she had courageously overcome her long-standing fear of driving, reclaiming her mobility and reshaping her life. Similarly, another individual in Bangladesh expressed gratitude, attributing their success in starting a farm business to the seeds of inspiration from our previous encounter.

These anecdotes serve as poignant reminders of the profound impact of self-motivation. They underscore the importance of taking ownership of one's journey, embracing challenges with resilience, and persistently pursuing one's goals. As I continue to encounter such stories, I am humbled by the realisation that self-motivation is not merely a fleeting sentiment but a potent catalyst for transformative change. By nurturing the flame of self-belief within us and others, we unlock untapped potential and embark on a journey of growth, empowerment, and fulfilment.

Self-motivation gives you the courage to bounce back from heartbreak and setbacks. Despite experiencing disappointment and shattered dreams when one of the companies I worked for closed due to circumstances not in my control, I realised the importance of not giving up. Instead of succumbing to despair, I faced the challenge head-on and explored new opportunities. Despite initially swearing off the industry, I eventually found myself drawn back to it, driven by a passion for positive discussions, leadership, and motivation. This journey taught me the value of perseverance and adaptability, showing that setbacks can be catalysts for growth and new beginnings. It's a reminder that despite adversity, staying resilient and open to new possibilities can lead to unexpected paths to success and fulfilment.

I recently reconnected with an acquaintance, almost a friend, in Pakistan. He told me the news of his recent accomplishment: completing his Ph.D. program. In our conversation, he attributed his success to the motivation he gained from our previous interactions.

However, I gently reminded him that the credit truly belongs to him for his determination and perseverance. He recounted how he abandoned his PhD pursuit nearly 15 years ago, but with renewed motivation, he overcame past obstacles to achieve his goal.

Fear often arises from feelings of unpreparedness or a lack of necessary skills to achieve our goals. However, by embracing the Effort Bank concept, we can view fear as a signal for skill acquisition rather than an insurmountable barrier.

This perspective shift encourages a focus on consistent effort and skill development, thereby reducing anxiety related to success or failure by valuing the journey over immediate results. Confronting fear head-on and acting, despite its presence, is a powerful antidote.

Through personal experiences and resilience, we learn that growth requires pushing beyond comfort zones and embracing uncertainty, turning setbacks into opportunities for learning and development.

Ultimately, self-motivation drives this process, empowering individuals to pursue their goals, overcome obstacles, and succeed persistently. Through the ripple effect of self-motivation, individuals fuel their growth and inspire others to do the same, fostering a culture of empowerment and possibility.

PART II:

UNLOCKING THE EFFORT BANK

IN THIS SECTION, I examine how you can effectively utilise the reserves within your Effort Bank, transforming the theoretical understanding into actionable steps. As conceptualised throughout our discussions, the Effort Bank symbolises the accumulated potential from our endeavours, learnings, and experiences—a vault waiting to be unlocked.

The leadership attitudes and skills I'm about to share are not just suggestions but essential keys to unlocking the vast potential stored within your Effort Bank. I've chosen these ten attitudes and skills for their critical role in navigating personal and professional growth avenues. Each one acts as a unique key, and as the vault of your Effort Bank expands, the need for more keys—more attitudes and skills—becomes apparent.

Remember, this journey is not a one-time event. It's a continuous cycle were engaging with your Effort Bank leads to personal growth, enlarging the vault and requiring an increasingly diverse set of skills for unlocking. As we progress, the vault's growth demands more from us regarding attitudes and abilities, solidifying our belief in the efficacy of the Effort Bank concept.

This section provides a practical roadmap for developing these leadership attitudes and skills, guiding you through personal and professional development aligned with the Effort Bank's principles. Through exploring these twenty keys, you're invited on a journey of continuous improvement and realising potential, all within the framework of unlocking your Effort Bank. You can trust in the practicality and effectiveness of this roadmap.

CHAPTER SIX

KEYS TO THE EFFORT BANK

AS WE CLOSED THE SECOND chapter, we laid the groundwork for understanding the Effort Bank—a repository where every endeavour, every learned lesson, and every ounce of perseverance is stored, amassing a wealth of potential ready for the right moment. With this foundation set, we venture into the second section with a burning question echoing in the minds of many: "I've been depositing for the last 20 years; how do I withdraw?"

This chapter is where the pathway becomes clear. It's designed to answer that pivotal question, unveiling how you can access the accumulated wealth within your Effort Bank. You've been making deposits for years—through challenges faced, skills honed, and resilience built. Now, the focus shifts to unlocking this vault and realising the value of those deposits in tangible, impactful ways.

Unlocking the Effort Bank isn't about finding a single key; it's about mastering a set of keys—each representing a leadership attitude or skill crucial for accessing your stored potential. These keys are not mere metaphors but practical attributes and competencies that enable you to open the vault and utilise its contents effectively.

This chapter explores these keys, understanding how each contributes to unlocking the Effort Bank. From resilience and adaptability to vision and passion, every key offers unique access to the vault, allowing you to draw from its depth and breadth. This journey through the keys is not just about personal enrichment but amplifying your impact, extending your influence, and achieving the goals that once seemed just out of reach.

So, as you stand before your Effort Bank, pondering over the years of deposits, this section lights the way forward. Here, you'll discover how to turn those deposits into dividends, transforming effort into achievement and potential into reality. Welcome to Chapter 6: Keys to the Vault, the beginning of your journey from depositing to withdrawing, from dreaming to doing.

First Deserve, Then Desire

"First deserve, then desire" is a principle we emphasise in our training, underscoring the necessity of being prepared for our aspirations. It raises a fundamental question: Are you ready for what you seek? For instance, if you aim to explore the ocean's depths through scuba diving, donning the appropriate suit and gear is essential—you must first be equipped to undertake the journey. Similarly, if your ambition is to reach the pinnacle of your field, possessing the requisite skills and attitude is non-negotiable. It would be best if you first merited the position you desire. This concept is encapsulated in the acronym ASK—Attitude, Skills, and Knowledge—a formula that suggests you shall receive only when you possess these critical attributes.

Cashing out or withdrawing from your Effort Bank further illustrates this principle. Consider the depiction of bank vaults in movies: the grander the vault, the more intricate the security. Like a hotel room safe, a small vault might require just a single key, and its contents are relatively modest. In contrast, a substantial bank vault, vast and fortified, necessitates numerous keys, reflecting the value and volume of its contents. This analogy highlights that the magnitude of your Effort Bank dictates the complexity of accessing it. An immense vault, symbolising a more significant accumulation of efforts and achievements, demands more keys for unlocking.

Therefore, if you wish to "cash out" from your Effort Bank, the scale of your withdrawal will depend on the size of your deposit. A minimal effort yields a smaller vault that is easily accessible but limited in reward. Conversely, a vault brimming with substantial efforts requires a more extensive set of keys to unlock. Regardless of the vault's size, even if small, opening it brings rewards proportional to the efforts stored within.

The core of this chapter lies in understanding that accumulating efforts in your Effort Bank and possessing the keys to access it—whether they number one or fifty—are fundamental to realising your desires.

This narrative encourages continuous contribution to your Effort Bank, for as it grows, so does the necessity for a broader array of keys, each symbolising the Attitude, Skills, and Knowledge required to achieve your ambitions.

Deserving Desire Through Dedication

Incorporating insights from the field of psychology, particularly the work of Carol Dweck on growth mindset, provides a deeper understanding of the "First Deserve, Then Desire" principle. Dweck's research underscores the importance of believing that our abilities and intelligence can be developed through hard work, perseverance, and dedication. This growth mindset is pivotal for anyone striving to make themselves deserving of their aspirations.

It encourages embracing challenges, persistence through difficulties, and a continuous journey of learning and self-improvement. Cultivating a growth mindset aligns perfectly with the ethos of preparing oneself to achieve desired goals, reinforcing that effort and attitude are crucial to unlocking one's potential.

Furthermore, the principle of "First Deserve, Then Desire" resonates with the concept of deliberate practice, a term popularised by psychologist Anders Ericsson. Deliberate practice involves focused, structured training to improve performance. This concept suggests that merely desiring success is not enough; one must engage in consistent, effortful, targeted actions to enhance specific skills and competencies. This aligns with the need for Attitude, Skills, and Knowledge (ASK) to access the Effort Bank, emphasising that achievement results from preparation and the willingness to engage in rigorous practice.

Lastly, leadership research highlights the significance of vision and passion in inspiring and guiding teams towards common goals. Leaders who articulate their vision and demonstrate passion inspire their team members and model the behaviour necessary to achieve collective aspirations. This dynamic further illustrates the "First Deserve, Then Desire" principle by showing that leadership requires a foundation of credibility and competence. Leaders earn the right to aspire and achieve through their dedication to growth, embodying the qualities they wish to see in their teams.

These insights from psychology, personal development, and leadership studies enrich our understanding of "First Deserve, Then Desire." They highlight the multifaceted approach needed to prepare oneself for achieving desired goals, emphasising that success is not merely about wanting but about becoming deserving through continuous effort, growth, and leadership.

ASK and You Shall Receive

(ASK: Attitude, Skills, and Knowledge)

To unlock the Effort Bank, we employ a three-pronged approach encapsulated by the acronym ASK—Attitude, Skills, and Knowledge. Each element of ASK plays a crucial role in accessing the Effort Bank and ensuring that we are fully prepared to leverage its contents to achieve our goals. Explore each component further and understand how they are foundational personal and professional growth pillars.

Attitude

The cornerstone of success, attitude, influences how we perceive challenges and opportunities. It shapes our resilience, willingness to embrace change, and ability to persist through adversity. A positive attitude fosters an environment where growth is not just a possibility but an expectation. It's about seeing the glass half full, finding solutions to problems, and viewing setbacks as stages of progress to more significant achievements. This mindset is vital for leaders who wish to inspire and motivate their teams towards shared goals, cultivating an atmosphere where collective effort and positivity drive progress.

A positive attitude involves a proactive and optimistic approach to depositing into and withdrawing from one's repository of efforts and achievements. It embodies the belief that every action taken, challenge faced, and lesson learned contributes valuable currency to the Effort Bank, which can be leveraged for future success. Here's how a positive attitude plays out concerning the Effort Bank:

A positive attitude shapes how individuals perceive and interact with the world, especially when building and leveraging their Effort Bank. It allows them to see every experience, particularly the challenging ones, as valuable additions to their reservoir of potential. Such a mindset reframes setbacks not as barriers but as opportunities for learning and growth, contributing to a more substantial foundation for future success.

When the time comes to cash out or apply the accumulated efforts toward achieving a specific goal, a positive attitude is instrumental. It provides the resilience necessary to navigate any challenges encountered in this process, bolstered by the belief that the required resources for success have already been secured within Effort Bank.

This outlook also fosters a mindset of continuous improvement, motivating individuals to keep adding to their Effort Bank through learning, personal development, and the pursuit of excellence. Every new skill or piece of knowledge gained increases their capacity to achieve their goals and enriches their journey.

A positive attitude is contagious in leadership, inspiring team members to mirror this outlook. Such collective positivity fosters a motivated, unified, and efficient team dynamic, with each member contributing to a shared Effort Bank and collaborating towards shared goals.

Adaptability to change is another facet enhanced by a positive mindset. It enables individuals to view new challenges not as threats but as opportunities to enrich their Effort Bank further. In today's ever-evolving landscape, this ability to adapt is invaluable, often determining one's capacity to succeed.

Lastly, embracing failure as a form of feedback is critical to maintaining a positive attitude. This perspective allows individuals to learn from their mistakes, thereby deepening their Effort Bank with refined strategies and improved approaches for future endeavours. A positive attitude nurtures personal growth and success and enhances the collective journey towards achieving shared objectives.

Skills

Leadership transcends vision; it necessitates the mastery of specific skills that bring that vision to life. Effective leadership is underpinned by skills essential for navigating the multifaceted challenges of guiding teams and achieving organisational objectives. These skills form the toolkit every leader needs to influence, inspire, and implement strategies successfully.

At the heart of leadership lies the art of goal setting, the practice of defining clear and achievable objectives that guide the direction of a team or organisation. Coupled with this is the critical skill of decision-making, where leaders must assess various alternatives and select the course of action that best aligns with their goals and values. Equally important is listening, which involves genuinely understanding the perspectives of others to build rapport and trust within a team.

Negotiation skills enable leaders to broker agreements that serve the interests of all parties involved. At the same time, public speaking allows them to inspire and engage audiences, rallying them behind a shared mission. Problem-solving is another crucial skill, enabling leaders to identify and implement solutions to challenges as they arise.

Communication plays a focal role, as it involves effectively conveying ideas and fostering an environment of open dialogue where all voices are heard. Effective leadership also requires time management and prioritising tasks to maximise productivity without compromising quality. Stress management is essential for maintaining composure and clarity under pressure, ensuring leaders can make sound decisions even in high-stress situations. Lastly, emotional intelligence skills are about understanding and managing your own emotions as well as the emotions of others. Leaders with high emotional intelligence can motivate teams, address emotional needs, and foster collaboration.

Together, these skills enable leaders to navigate the complexities of their roles effectively. They are not merely competencies to be learned but are integral to the practice of leadership, empowering leaders to guide their teams with confidence and achieve the strategic objectives of their organisations. By developing and refining these skills, leaders can ensure they are well-equipped to turn their vision into reality, fostering an environment where success is envisioned and realised.

The detailed examination in Chapter 8 will further equip readers with the knowledge and tools necessary to master these skills, paving the way for leadership that transcends mere management to inspire and effect change truly.

Polishing the Diamonds in Your Effort Bank

Polishing the diamonds in your Effort Bank is a metaphor for refining and enhancing the skills and qualities contributing to your success and resilience in facing challenges. These "diamonds" represent your inherent talents, learned skills, experiences, and the efforts you've invested over time. Just as diamonds require cutting and polishing to reveal their brilliance, your abilities and efforts need continuous development and refinement to shine. Here are seven diamonds that serve as crucial elements in this polishing process:

1. **Adaptability**

Adjusting your strategies, goals, or approaches in response to changing circumstances is crucial. Adaptability ensures you can navigate unexpected challenges and take advantage of new opportunities. It is an essential skill in both personal development and professional growth, embodying the capacity to adjust to new conditions, challenges, and opportunities with flexibility and resourcefulness. Adaptability has become more valuable in an ever-changing world marked by rapid technological advancements, shifting societal norms, and unpredictable economic landscapes. It enables individuals to thrive in diverse environments, embrace change positively, and pivot when necessary to seize new opportunities or address unforeseen challenges.

At its core, adaptability is about being open to change and ready to evolve in response to external circumstances. This does not mean being aimless or lacking in principle; instead, it involves having a solid foundation of values and goals while being flexible in the methods used to achieve them. Adaptable individuals can reassess their strategies, learn new skills, and modify their approaches in the face of new information or changing conditions.

Adaptability is a cornerstone of resilience, empowering individuals to overcome adversity by identifying alternative routes to their goals. This quality enables one to navigate setbacks and fosters a mindset oriented towards continuous learning and growth. As adaptable people view every change as a chance to learn something new, they embody the essence of lifelong learning, constantly evolving in their personal and professional lives.

Moreover, adaptability enhances problem-solving capabilities by encouraging creative and innovative thinking. Adaptable individuals are adept at considering challenges from various angles, allowing them to devise unique solutions. This trait also improves interpersonal relationships and team dynamics; adaptable people tend to be more collaborative and empathetic, understanding and accommodating different perspectives and working styles, which fosters a harmonious and productive environment.

Cultivating adaptability involves embracing a proactive and flexible mindset grounded in the belief that one's abilities and intelligence can grow through dedication, effort, and experiential learning. Viewing challenges as opportunities rather than obstacles is critical, as is the willingness to regularly step out of your comfort zone by engaging in new situations that demand adaptation—assuming different roles in projects, acquiring new skills, or altering daily routines.

A relentless curiosity about the world, people, and novel experiences fosters this adaptability, encouraging an openness that naturally leads to a more adaptable life approach. Reflecting on each significant experience or challenge, assessing what was learned, how one adapted, and considering alternative approaches for the future further solidifies this adaptable mindset, making it a powerful tool for personal and professional development.

2. Continuous Learning

Continuous learning is an essential development strategy, enabling individuals to remain competitive and relevant in an ever-changing world. This pursuit involves a proactive approach to acquiring new knowledge, skills, and insights, which can significantly enhance one's capabilities and adaptability.

It is about maintaining a mindset open to new ideas, experiences, and perspectives. It requires an individual to actively seek growth opportunities through formal education, professional training, or self-directed learning endeavours. This could include enrolling in courses, attending workshops, participating in webinars, or engaging with online educational platforms.

Moreover, continuous learning extends beyond traditional educational settings. It involves seeking feedback and constructive criticism from peers, mentors, and supervisors, which can provide valuable insights into areas for improvement. Engaging in new experiences, taking on challenging projects, and stepping out of one's comfort zone are critical components of this learning process. These experiences contribute to skill development and enhance one's ability to think critically and solve problems creatively.

In addition to personal growth, continuous learning plays a crucial role in professional advancement. By staying abreast of their field's latest trends, technologies, and methodologies, individuals can position themselves as valuable assets to their organisations. This commitment to ongoing education signals a dedication to excellence and a willingness to contribute to the success of their team and the broader industry.

Ultimately, it is a lifelong journey that enriches the mind and the career. It fosters resilience, encourages innovation, and prepares individuals to face the complexities of the modern world with confidence and competence. By embracing continuous learning, one can unlock new opportunities, achieve personal fulfilment, and make a lasting impact in their chosen field.

3. Self-Reflection

Self-reflection is a powerful ability that mirrors our inner selves and clarifies our thoughts, behaviours, and decisions. This reflective process allows individuals to consider their experiences—both successes and failures—critically and objectively, fostering a deeper understanding of their motivations, strengths, weaknesses, and the outcomes of their actions.

Through self-reflection, one can identify patterns in their behaviour that may contribute to their successes or setbacks. This awareness is crucial for personal development, as it highlights improvement areas and helps set more realistic goals. By examining the decisions that led to specific outcomes, individuals can learn valuable lessons, adjust their strategies, and make more informed choices in the future.

Additionally, self-reflection encourages emotional intelligence by enhancing one's ability to understand and manage emotions. Recognising how emotions influence decisions and interactions with others can lead to better communication, stronger relationships, and more effective problem-solving skills. This reflective practice also contributes to resilience, as it helps individuals to process and learn from their experiences, including failures and challenges, viewing them as opportunities for growth rather than insurmountable obstacles.

Engaging in regular self-reflection requires discipline and honesty. It can be facilitated through various practices, such as journaling, meditation, or engaging in thoughtful discussions with mentors or peers. These activities provide a structured framework for examining one's thoughts and actions, giving a clearer perspective on personal values, goals, and the steps needed to achieve them.

Self-reflection is about pausing, looking inward, and assessing one's life path and the choices that have shaped it. By regularly engaging in this practice, individuals can cultivate a more profound sense of self-awareness, guiding their future actions and personal growth in a more intentional and informed direction. This continuous cycle of action, reflection, and adaptation is essential for achieving lasting personal development and fulfilment.

4. Knowledge

Understanding the domain in which you operate is crucial for making informed decisions and leading confidently. In leadership, knowledge plays a pivotal role in shaping decisions and guiding actions with confidence. It's the foundation upon which informed strategies are built and innovative solutions are crafted.

However, knowledge extends far beyond the mere accumulation of information; it encompasses a deep understanding of the nuances and dynamics within one's domain. This understanding is crystallised through the mastery of what can be referred to as the four Cs:

1. Critical thinking
2. Creativity
3. Collaboration, and
4. Communication.

Each of these facets contributes to a leader's ability to navigate the complexities of their environment and steer their team towards success.

Critical thinking is the skill of meticulously analysing situations to form reasoned judgments. It involves evaluating information from various sources, identifying biases, and considering different perspectives before making decisions. This analytical approach ensures that leaders are not merely reacting to the surface-level symptoms of challenges but are addressing their underlying causes with well-thought-out strategies. It's about asking the right questions, challenging assumptions, and foreseeing potential impacts, which are essential for navigating the intricate landscapes of modern industries.

Creativity builds on this foundation by encouraging leaders to think outside the conventional paradigms and explore new avenues for problem-solving. It's about innovating and imagining possibilities that have not yet been realised. In today's rapidly evolving world, the ability to adapt and innovate is not just valuable; it's necessary for survival. Creativity empowers leaders to develop unique solutions to complex problems, fostering a culture of innovation within their teams and organisations.

Collaboration is equally crucial, emphasising the importance of working effectively with others to achieve shared objectives. The complexity and scale of challenges organisations face today require a collective effort to overcome. Collaboration is about harnessing each team member's diverse skills, perspectives, and strengths, creating a synergistic force capable of achieving far more than any individual could. It involves building trust, fostering open communication, and creating an inclusive environment where everyone feels valued and empowered to contribute.

Finally, **Communication** ties all these elements together, enhancing the leader's ability to share ideas, insights, and visions effectively. It's not just about transmitting information but about ensuring it is understood, appreciated, and acted upon by others. Effective communication bridges the gap between knowledge and action, facilitating clear understanding and alignment within the team. It involves listening actively, expressing ideas clearly, and engaging in meaningful dialogues that drive progress.

Together, these four Cs form a comprehensive framework for knowledge in leadership, enabling leaders to adapt, innovate, and thrive in an ever-changing global landscape. By cultivating these key areas, leaders can gain a deeper understanding of their industry, navigate market dynamics skilfully, and lead their teams with an informed and inspiring vision.

The pathway to accessing the Effort Bank becomes evident, demanding the ambition to succeed and the readiness to harness that ambition effectively. Through exploring ASK—Attitude, Skills, and Knowledge—we've uncovered what it truly means to equip ourselves for the achievements we seek. A positive attitude establishes the foundation, igniting our motivation and resilience. The ten essential leadership skills provide us with the tools to navigate our roles' intricacies, enabling us to actualise our visions. Knowledge, enriched by critical thinking, creativity, collaboration, and communication, prepares us to make informed decisions and lead with assurance.

This chapter has presented the keys to unlocking the Effort Bank, highlighting that accessing our stored efforts and accomplishments is determined by our preparedness to utilise them. The ASK framework extends beyond mere advice; it is imperative for ongoing personal and professional development, encouraging us to invest in our growth and capabilities.

Let this information be the groundwork upon which we build our aspirations. Exploration, challenges, and triumphs mark the road ahead. Equipped with the correct attitude, skills, and knowledge, no vault is too fortified, and no objective is too remote. The keys are within our grasp, and the moment to act is now. Let's proceed with the assurance that we are prepared to unlock our Effort Bank and ready to achieve the success we've diligently worked toward. The path to unlocking our full potential may be demanding, but it is achievable for those who are determined to pursue it.

CHAPTER SEVEN

LEADERSHIP ATTITUDE

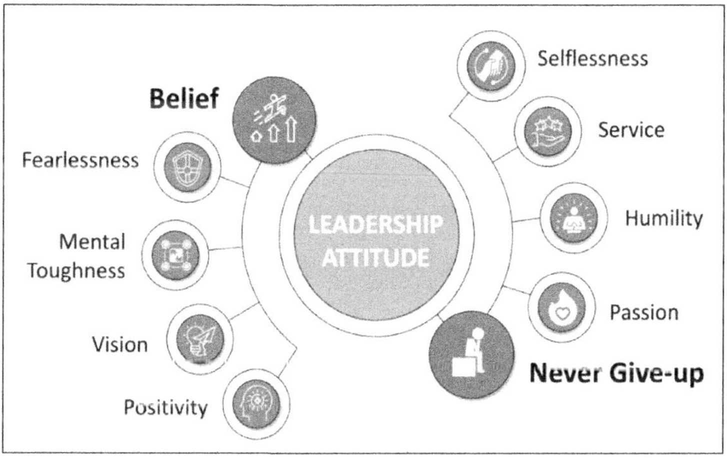

THIS BOOK UNVEILS THE Effort Bank, a unique concept that serves as a metaphorical vault for everyone's potential and accomplishments. We delve into the process of unlocking this reservoir, underscoring that a more substantial Effort Bank necessitates a greater number of keys for access. These keys, which are symbolic of attitudes and skills, hold the power to unlock one's full potential.

My personal journey in leadership has taught me more than just skills and knowledge. It's been a transformative experience, shaping how I navigate challenges, influence others, and maintain resilience in the face of adversity. Embracing a Leadership Attitude, I've learned to spot opportunities within obstacles, foster growth amidst uncertainty, and rally a unified vision against scepticism.

This approach integrates resilience, empathy, determination, humility, vision, and pragmatism. This chapter will illustrate how such an attitude can turn potential into action, using leadership as a catalyst for achieving unparalleled success in the Effort Bank.

We'll explore the critical aspects of Leadership Attitude, including belief, fearlessness, mental toughness, vision, positivity, never giving up, passion, humility, service and selflessness. As we'll see, authentic leadership isn't about wielding power but empowering others. Join me in this exploration of Leadership Attitude, where we chart the journey from effort to impact, starting with the cornerstone of Belief.

1) Belief

In this first topic, we're sharing the importance of belief in whatever you're doing, whether it's a project, your business, or your job. Having belief is crucial. If you're leading a team or a group, your belief in yourself, your team, and the company's vision and mission is vital. A leader's belief makes a significant difference because if the leader lacks belief in their actions, the team descends into chaos, losing sight of the big picture.

This lack of vision prevents the team from exerting effort and energy to achieve the larger goal. It would be best to believe that persistently doing the right things will eventually lead to achieving your goals. I often talk about the "Effort Bank." Believing in the Effort Bank can help you overcome obstacles and challenges, encouraging you to take massive action toward success. Let's recap the Effort Bank a bit.

I shared the story of Ali, Ben, and Charlie. For context, Ali, Ben, and Charlie have identical backgrounds in terms of education, socioeconomic status, and skills. The assumption is that Ali, Ben, and Charlie are at the same level, coming from the same background and having identical skills and education. Ali's story illustrates the number of efforts (depicted by yellow boxes) he put into his job or business and the returns he received (shown in red boxes).

Despite increasing his efforts, he saw diminishing returns. Eventually, Ali decided to minimise his losses by reducing his efforts, which paradoxically led to some success. On the other hand, Ben sees equal rewards for his efforts, which Ali envies, attributing Ben's success to luck. Then there's Charlie, who exerts minimal effort but receives massive rewards.

Story of Ali, Ben & Charlie

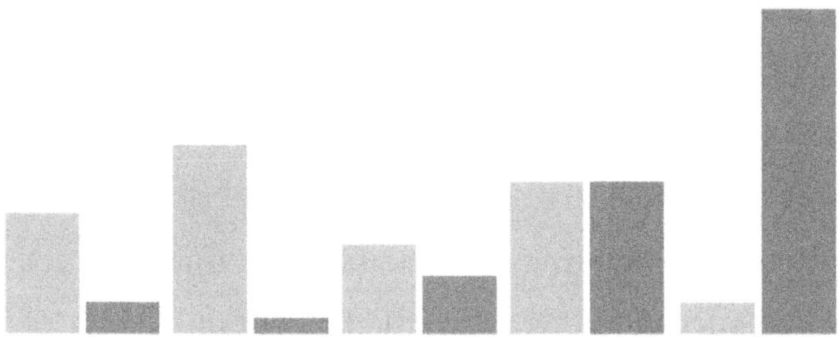

Ali and Ben aspire to be like Charlie, believing him exceptionally lucky. However, Ali's unrewarded efforts (shown in blue boxes) are well-spent; they accumulate in the Effort Bank. When the time is right, the Effort Bank rewards past efforts. Essentially, Ali, Ben, and Charlie represent different phases in the same person's life, highlighting the cycle of effort and reward. This concept underlines the importance of depositing efforts into the Effort Bank to unlock future success, which may seem like luck to outsiders.

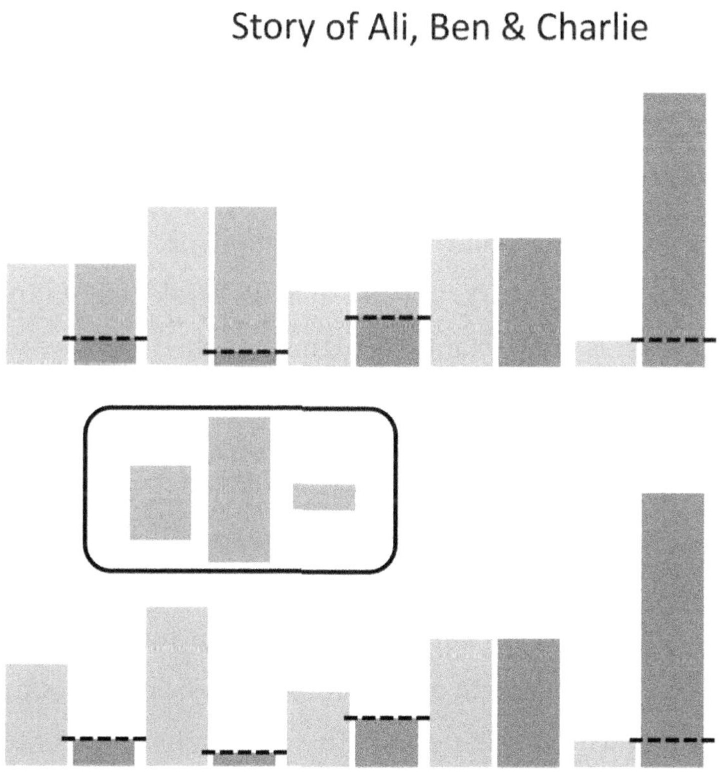

This also ties into a personal anecdote involving a restaurant owner and his son, illustrating the impact of belief and perception on success. The son, taking over the restaurant with caution, advised by his dying father, reduces orders to save costs.

While initially seeming prudent, this decision leads to decreased customer satisfaction and, eventually, the restaurant's closure. This story exemplifies how positive or negative beliefs can significantly influence outcomes and manifest, reinforcing the importance of maintaining a positive outlook and belief system.

The action point for this section on belief is to celebrate hard work, not just success. While celebrating success is important, recognising the hard work behind it is crucial. Even if immediate success is not evident, the effort is stored in your Effort Bank for future rewards.

Belief in Career

Belief in one's career is a powerful force shaping professional growth and fulfilment trajectory. It is the confidence to pursue a path that aligns with one's passions and strengths, even when it diverges from conventional expectations.

This belief fuels persistence through challenges and setbacks, encouraging continuous learning and adaptation in an ever-changing work environment. It empowers individuals to advocate for themselves, seek out opportunities that resonate with their ambitions, and embrace the risks associated with career advancement. Belief in one's career potential fosters resilience, enabling professionals to rebound from failures with greater insight and determination. Ultimately, this deep-seated belief turns aspirations into accomplishments, guiding individuals to achieve their career goals and redefine their sense of purpose and success in the workplace.

Belief in Business

Belief in business is more than just a strategic advantage; it's the engine that drives innovation, resilience, and growth. It starts with the conviction in a vision that can reshape markets, influence customer behaviours, and redefine what's possible.

This foundational belief inspires leaders and entrepreneurs to pursue audacious goals, navigate uncertainties, and make decisions that may seem risky to outsiders. It compels a start-up to challenge giants, a local business to envision a global presence, and a struggling company to pivot towards unprecedented success.

In business, belief acts as both a shield and a catalyst, protecting the core mission during tough times while pushing boundaries to explore new opportunities. Ultimately, belief in business transforms the intangible into tangible success, turning dreams into realities and aspirations into achievements.

Belief in Self

Belief in oneself is the bedrock upon which all personal triumphs are built. The quiet assurance whispers in moments of doubt, propelling us forward when the path ahead seems clouded. This intrinsic faith acts as the compass guiding us through life's challenges, illuminating our capabilities and potential even when they're obscured by failure or criticism.

When we foster a deep, unwavering belief in our abilities, we unlock a reservoir of inner strength, enabling us to face adversity with resilience, pursue our goals with unrelenting determination, and open ourselves to growth and learning. In essence, self-belief is not just about achieving what we set out to do; it's about discovering who we are and the heights we can reach when we trust our power to overcome and succeed.

I urge you to reflect on the power of belief and the invaluable lessons learned from Ali, Ben, Charlie, and the restaurant owner. These stories highlight the importance of persistence and perspective and remind us that our beliefs shape our reality. Celebrating hard work, maintaining a positive outlook, and understanding the role of timing and effort are key to unlocking the potential within each of us and achieving our goals.

Locus of Control

Locus of control has always been a concept that fascinates me, both in how it shapes our personal lives and in its implications for the business world. At its core, it's about how much I control the events that affect me. Reflecting on my own experiences, I recognise moments where having an internal locus of control empowered me, driving me to act and believe in my ability to influence outcomes. Conversely, I've also felt the weight of an external locus of control, a sense of helplessness in the face of external forces, whether chance, fate, or the actions of others.

I've observed that people generally fall into two categories: those with a highly external locus of control and those with an extremely internal one. Individuals with an external locus of control often feel helpless about their future, lamenting, "Why does everything happen to me? Why bother when nothing is working? It's all wrong." They attribute their circumstances to external factors—blaming their situation on others, their environment, or societal forces such as politics or the economy. This mindset, a highly external locus of control, externalises responsibility.

Conversely, those with a highly internal locus of control internalise too much, believing any misfortune is due to their shortcomings. They might think, "I'm just bad luck," or "It's all my fault. I'm no good, and nothing I attempt ever works out." This perspective signifies an internal locus of control, where individuals blame themselves for every mishap, often unjustly.

However, neither extreme is conducive to a healthy or productive mindset. I advocate for a balanced internal locus of control. This balanced approach lets us say, "I can build my future. Let me try." When we achieve even a small success, we can proudly acknowledge, "Look what I can do. I make things happen." This mindset recognises internal and external factors but emphasises personal agency and responsibility without dismissing the impact of external circumstances. Essentially, the mantra of someone with a balanced internal locus of control is, "I make things happen."

In my training, I often incorporate interactive elements by posing questions to the participants. While translating this experience to a book format may pose a challenge, other authors successfully engage readers by asking questions and providing space for personal reflection.

For instance, I might ask, "What is your locus of control? Is it extremely internal, extremely external, or balanced towards an internal locus where you feel empowered to make things happen?"

I reinforce the message of every topic discussed in this chapter on leadership attitudes with a personal motto. For belief, it is: "Your efforts are always rewarded. You may get paid now or later but remember the Effort Bank. Don't fret over the results; continue to work hard." This encapsulates maintaining a balanced locus of control and the importance of perseverance and belief in oneself.

In life, embracing an internal locus of control is transformative. It leads to adopting a proactive approach to challenges, instilling a belief that efforts and decisions directly impact success and happiness. This mindset encourages responsibility and self-reflection, pushing us to learn from our mistakes and celebrate victories as products of our making. It's not about ignoring the randomness of life or the impact of external factors but rather focusing on how we respond to them, which is a powerful form of control.

Transitioning this perspective to the business realm, I have observed how a collective internal locus of control within a team or organisation can drive success. It fosters a culture of accountability and empowerment, where individuals feel motivated to contribute their best efforts because they believe in their capacity to make a difference.

This leads to higher engagement, innovation, and resilience, as everyone from the top-down takes ownership of their roles and work outcomes. It starkly contrasts environments where an external locus of control prevails, often characterised by blame-shifting, passivity, and a lack of initiative.

However, balancing this mindset is crucial. Acknowledging external factors—market trends, regulatory changes, and competitive actions—and adapting strategies accordingly is essential. The key is not to feel victimised by these externalities but to consider them variables in the decision-making equation. This balanced approach, integrating an internal locus of control with a realistic appraisal of external factors, guides me in navigating the complexities of business strategy and operations.

In sum, locus of control is a lens through which we view challenges and opportunities in our lives and professional activities. It shapes your interactions, decisions, leadership, and personal development philosophy. By consciously cultivating an internal locus of control while remaining mindful of the forces beyond your influence, you navigate life's unpredictabilities with a sense of agency and purpose.

2. Fearlessness

This quality is essential in our discussion on fearlessness, particularly in leadership. Without fearlessness, making tough decisions and taking calculated risks—which I delve into in another chapter on decision-making—becomes nearly impossible. Fearlessness equips leaders to face challenges head-on, remain receptive to feedback, and learn from failures. Importantly, being fearless doesn't mean being devoid of fear; it's about harnessing courage to act despite fear. In this framework, courage is the willingness to embrace uncertainty, propelling us towards action and success.

I remember vividly my first public presentation. Like anyone else, I was nervous; my stomach was in knots, and I momentarily forgot my name as I stepped onto the stage. After countless presentations, I've improved, but it would be misleading to claim that I'm now without fear. The butterflies haven't disappeared; what's changed is my ability to manage them. Managing fear, rather than eliminating it, is vital. Bethany Hamilton, a professional surfer whose story is both harrowing and inspiring, perfectly captures this sentiment. Despite losing her arm to a shark attack, she didn't let fear or the incident halt her passion for surfing. Her courage and determination to not let fear deter her path is a powerful testament to fearlessness.

Living in constant fear holds us back. Whether it's fear of job loss, relationship issues, or business failures, breaking free from the chains of fear is crucial. A thought exercise I find helpful is to define what courage means to you personally. This reflection can be a potent reminder of your resilience and strength.

Managing fear is a practical skill that can be honed. Before acting—regardless of the scale of the decision—the question of whether it's the right choice often paralyses us. However, the fear of making a wrong decision should not deter action. A bad decision can yield valuable experience, just as a right one can lead to success. Either outcome contributes to our "Effort Bank," enriching our understanding and informing future decisions. Success isn't just about the immediate outcome but also about accumulating experiences that shape our journey.

Mastering fear management is a pivotal element in personal and professional development. Fear, inherently woven into the fabric of our emotional response system, is a double-edged sword. While it has evolved to protect us from imminent dangers, signalling when to fight or flee, it can also immobilise us, clouding our judgment and preventing us from seizing opportunities beyond our comfort zones. To navigate this landscape, a nuanced understanding of fear and practical strategies for its management is indispensable.

Managing fear commences with a deep dive into its origins. Fear often springs from a complex interplay of internal beliefs and external situations. It reflects our deepest vulnerabilities, anxieties, and, sometimes, irrational apprehensions about the future. Identifying and pinpointing the exact source of fear is akin to mapping the terrain of a known enemy. Acknowledging its presence becomes the next critical step once the contours of fear are laid bare. This process of acknowledgement, devoid of any self-judgment, is liberating. It diminishes the shackles of fear, giving a clearer perspective on the challenges ahead.

Fear manifests through a spectrum of physical and emotional symptoms, each signalling the body's reaction to perceived threats. The heart races, palms sweat, and muscles tense, preparing the body for action. These physical signs are the body's ancient alarm system, yet in modern contexts, they often precede not physical danger but emotional and psychological battles. Similarly, fear stirs a whirlwind of emotions — anxiety, frustration, a sense of being overwhelmed — each amplifying the original fear. Recognising these signs and emotions as mere responses to fear rather than insurmountable truths paves the way for effective management strategies.

Breathing techniques and mindfulness practices are among the most potent tools against fear. Deep, controlled breathing acts as a bridge to calmness, guiding the nervous system to a state of equilibrium and diffusing the immediate intensity of fear's physical symptoms. On the other hand, mindfulness and meditation extend an invitation to observe one's thoughts and feelings with detachment. This practice fosters an environment where fear can be examined without being reacted to impulsively. It encourages curiosity and openness towards fear rather than avoidance or denial.

Individuals can gracefully navigate the turbulent waters of fear by implementing these strategies. The path to managing fear is not about eradicating it; instead, it's about developing a relationship with fear that acknowledges its presence but refuses to let it steer the course of one's life. Through understanding, acceptance, and strategic action, fear transforms from a formidable foe into a manageable aspect of the human experience, one that can even catalyse growth, resilience, and a deeper engagement with life's myriad opportunities.

Embracing Fearlessness

Embracing fearlessness means understanding that both success and failure are integral to growth. The mantra that guides me in this context is: "Falling and standing up is the sign of courage." It represents a profound shift in how we engage with one of our most primal emotions; rather than viewing fear as an adversary to be conquered or suppressed, embracing fear involves recognising it as an integral part of the human experience, one that can offer profound insights into our deepest desires, values, and the boundaries of our comfort zones.

This approach does not suggest that we seek out fear for fear's sake but rather that we learn to see fear as a signal, guiding us toward areas of potential growth and learning.

It's a deliberate choice to live boldly, not in the absence of fear but in the mastery of it. Embracing fearlessness doesn't mean we no longer feel fear; rather, it signifies our commitment not to let fear dictate our decisions and limit our potential. This mindset cultivates a life rich in experiences, learning, and growth, marked by the courage to pursue our highest aspirations despite the risks involved.

The crux of incorporating fearlessness lies in recognising fear as a natural part of the human condition, a signal alerting us to risks and opportunities for significant growth and achievement. It requires a nuanced understanding that true bravery isn't about eradicating fear but facing it head-on with determination and resolve. This approach fosters an environment where we're encouraged to step out of our comfort zones, explore uncharted territories, and embrace the possibilities of taking calculated risks.

Central to a fearless life is developing a mindset that views challenges as stepping stones rather than obstacles. This perspective helps us reframe our experiences, seeing setbacks not as failures but as invaluable lessons that pave the way for future successes. By adopting this outlook, we cultivate resilience, enabling us to bounce back from adversities stronger and more equipped to handle the twists and turns of our journey.

Moreover, embracing fearlessness enriches our character, imbuing us with the confidence to stand up for our beliefs and values in the face of opposition. It inspires us to lead by example, demonstrating to others that it's possible to live authentically and pursue one's dreams, regardless of the fear of judgment or failure. This leadership by example has a ripple effect, empowering those around us to embrace a more fearless approach to life.

Living fearlessly opens the door to a deeper level of creativity and innovation. When we're not constrained by the fear of criticism or the dread of making mistakes, we're more likely to think outside the box, experiment with new ideas, and discover solutions that push the boundaries of what's possible. This creative freedom is essential for personal development and progress in any field or effort.

Ultimately, embracing fearlessness means forging a life that reflects our true potential and deepest desires. It's about consciously pursuing our goals with vigour and enthusiasm, even amid uncertainty and risk. Embracing fearlessness means living with purpose, passion, and perseverance, qualities that enable us to navigate the complexities of life with grace and confidence. It's a journey that challenges us to grow, learn, and thrive, transforming our fears into fuel for a fulfilling and meaningful life.

3. Mental Toughness

The next topic, or the key to unlocking your Effort Bank, is mental toughness. This entails being mentally strong and resilient, akin to having a rhinoceros'

skin—so thick that not even bullets can penetrate. Becoming mentally tough means you are determined to face challenges and adversity without being derailed from your goals. You remain calm and composed, even under high pressure. Sometimes, facing tight deadlines propels me to work more efficiently, allowing me to achieve my goals faster.

Venturing into uncharted waters can be daunting, but with mental fortitude, you can endure the pain and eventually achieve epic success. The greater the goal, the more challenging the grind. I introduce the concept of "grind is good" in this chapter, which we will explore further.

At the heart of mental toughness is the ability to remain calm and composed under pressure. It's about managing your emotions, so they don't overpower your ability to think clearly and make reasoned decisions. This control is essential for facing a critical moment in a sporting event, a high-stakes business negotiation, or a personal crisis. Mental toughness allows you to see beyond the immediate discomfort and focus on the bigger picture, maintaining your drive towards long-term goals.

One example is the story of Angry Birds. Many of you have likely played the Angry Birds game on your phones or computers. The company behind it, founded in 2003 by three individuals, created 51 games over six years. Despite their efforts, these games did not achieve commercial success, and by 2009, the company was nearly bankrupt. The three colleagues, barely managing to pay the bills and on the brink of bankruptcy, decided to try it again. Their mental toughness allowed them to endure the challenges they faced. They developed one more game, including the Angry Bird sketch, leading to its incredible success.

A favourite quote from Muhammad Ali, which I've cherished since I was young, perfectly encapsulates this idea of mental toughness. Ali said he doesn't count his sit-ups; he only starts counting when it hurts because that's when it counts. This quote reminds me that pain and struggle are not indicators of failure but growth and strength building. Whether in sports, like my own experience in Taekwondo, or in the natural world, such as a butterfly emerging from its cocoon, enduring pain and struggle is essential for growth. The butterfly must struggle to break free from its cocoon to strengthen its wings for flight. Similarly, bodybuilders don't achieve their physique overnight; it takes consistent effort and endurance through pain.

Awareness of your emotional graph is crucial, especially if you are not mentally tough. Successes can send you soaring, while failures can plunge you into doubt. Many give up after facing setbacks, but it's essential to manage these emotional fluctuations and persevere. Understanding and navigating this emotional graph is critical, as the initial 90 days of any new endeavour can be particularly turbulent. Expanding your comfort zone is also vital for growth. Success lies beyond our comfort zones, requiring continuous learning and effort expansion. However, it's essential to expand gradually to avoid burnout. Reflecting on the challenges and recognising that the grind is good can be profoundly rewarding.

Another critical aspect of mental toughness is the capacity for self-belief and confidence, even when external circumstances suggest otherwise. This unshakeable faith in your abilities propels you forward, motivating you to take on challenges others might shy away from. This isn't about arrogance or a denial of one's limitations; instead, it's a realistic assessment of your strengths and a determination to apply them effectively.

Mental toughness also involves a high degree of resilience—the ability to bounce back from failures, learn from mistakes, and continue striving towards your objectives. It's recognising that setbacks are not permanent or defining but are, instead, valuable learning opportunities. This resilience differentiates those who ultimately succeed from those who give up in the face of difficulty.

Steps to Achieve Mental Toughness

Achieving mental toughness is akin to embarking on a journey of self-discovery and resilience, a transformative process that fortifies the mind against life's inevitable challenges and setbacks. At its core, mental toughness involves cultivating a mindset that embraces growth, resilience, and persistence, enabling individuals to navigate adversity with strength and confidence. While deeply personal and unique to everyone, this journey follows a series of steps to develop a robust mental fortitude.

The first step in achieving mental toughness is to set clear, achievable goals. These goals act as beacons of light on the path, providing direction and a sense of purpose. Establishing what you want to achieve creates a roadmap for your journey, allowing you to focus your efforts and measure your progress. Goals should be challenging yet realistic, pushing you out of your comfort zone while ensuring they are attainable with hard work and dedication.

Embracing a growth mindset is another crucial step. This means viewing challenges and failures not as insurmountable obstacles or reflections of your innate abilities but as opportunities for learning and growth. Adopting this mindset encourages resilience as you begin to see setbacks as part of the learning process rather than reasons to give up. It fosters a sense of perseverance, urging you to continue pushing forward even when the going gets tough.

Building mental toughness also requires practising self-discipline. This involves developing routines and habits that support your goals and committing to them even when motivation wanes. Self-discipline is about making choices that align with your long-term objectives, even if they are not the most appealing or easy. Daily commitment to your goals builds the foundation of mental toughness, turning challenges into stepping stones towards your ultimate success.

Another critical element is fostering a positive attitude. This doesn't mean ignoring reality or pretending that difficulties don't exist. Instead, it's about maintaining a hopeful outlook, focusing on solutions rather than dwelling on problems. A positive attitude helps you remain resilient, enabling you to bounce back from setbacks with renewed vigour and determination.

Seeking support from others can significantly enhance your journey towards mental toughness. Whether it's friends, family, mentors, or a professional coach, having a support network provides encouragement, perspective, and accountability. Sharing your challenges and successes with others can also remind you that you're not alone in your journey, providing additional motivation and inspiration to continue striving towards your goals.

Achieving mental toughness is a gradual process that requires patience, commitment, and self-reflection. By setting clear goals, embracing a growth mindset, practising self-discipline, maintaining a positive attitude, and seeking support, you can build the resilience and strength to face life's challenges with confidence and grace. This journey enhances your ability to cope with adversity and leads to personal growth and fulfilment, making you stronger and more capable in every aspect of your life.

Cultivating mental toughness is a continuous process that requires practice and dedication. It involves developing a growth mindset, seeing abilities as malleable rather than fixed, and learning to approach challenges with optimism and persistence. It also means building a supportive network that encourages and challenges you while caring for your physical health to support your mental resilience.

4. Vision

Vision is the ability to envisage a future state or goal for you or your team that others might not see, which is crucial for leadership. Having a vision allows leaders to inspire and motivate themselves and their team, guiding them towards a common goal. I firmly believe that effective leadership is only possible with a clear vision. One of my favourite quotes by Ratan Tata exemplifies this: "I don't believe in taking the right decisions; I take decisions and then make them right." Some might perceive this as arrogance, but I see it as a testament to the courage to make decisions aligned with a vision driving towards success.

In leadership and business, vision is equally critical. It encapsulates a leader's or an organisation's aspirations for the future, outlining a clear and compelling picture of what success looks like. A strong vision provides a foundation for strategic planning, setting the stage for innovation and growth. It serves to rally employees, stakeholders, and customers around a common purpose, fostering a sense of belonging and commitment.

Visionary leadership involves having a clear vision and the ability to communicate it effectively and inspire others to embrace it. Leaders with vision are forward-thinking, seeing beyond the immediate to anticipate changes and opportunities on the horizon. They possess the creativity to imagine possibilities that others cannot and the courage to take calculated risks to turn those possibilities into reality.

This concept reminds me of a plane expedition. Contrary to what one might expect, a plane does not fly in a straight line from origin to destination. Instead, it sometimes takes off in a different direction, making numerous course corrections to its final goal. This process mirrors the importance of making decisions and adjusting them as necessary to stay aligned with one's vision.

For individuals, having a vision is about understanding where you want to go, what you aspire to achieve, and who you want to become. It's a source of motivation and a beacon during times of uncertainty or challenge. Personal vision acts as a compass, helping one navigate life's complexities and make decisions aligned with one's deepest values and desires.

Acquiring a vision requires introspection, imagination, and an understanding of one's environment and the forces that shape it. It involves considering future trends, societal changes, and technological advancements and integrating these insights with values and objectives. Whether personal or organisational, vision is not static; it evolves with time, reflecting new learnings, experiences, and circumstances.

I developed the concept of the "vision box" over the years, contrasting it with the "satisfaction box." The vision box is filled with future aspirations and a clear sense of direction, whereas the satisfaction box is riddled with doubts and uncertainties. A predominant satisfaction box can stifle one's vision, indicating a need to focus more on vision and less on immediate contentment.

Reflecting on vision in practice, consider the effort versus reward principle. Condensing 30 years of effort into three years can yield the same rewards but grants you 27 additional years. This approach demands a vision to recognise the long-term benefits of intensified effort.

5. Positivity

Positivity as a leadership attitude seamlessly intertwines with Effort Bank, shaping a dynamic framework for personal and professional growth. Leaders who embody positivity inspire and empower their teams to navigate challenges with resilience and determination. This attitude fosters an environment where individuals feel valued, supported, and motivated to invest their efforts wholeheartedly, knowing their contributions are essential to the collective success.

Leaders who maintain a positive outlook reinforce the belief that consistent action leads to long-term rewards. By encouraging their teams to approach tasks with optimism and enthusiasm, leaders create a culture where challenges are viewed as opportunities for growth rather than obstacles.

Moreover, positivity enhances collaboration and teamwork within organisations, essential components of maximising the impact of effort. Leaders who foster a positive work environment cultivate strong relationships built on trust, respect, and mutual support. This collaborative spirit fuels creativity, innovation, and a sense of camaraderie among team members.

As leaders model positivity in their actions and interactions, they inspire others to adopt a similar mindset, amplifying optimism throughout the organisation. By championing positivity as a core leadership trait, leaders cultivate a culture where individuals feel empowered to overcome obstacles, embrace challenges, and strive for excellence in their endeavours.

6. Never Give Up

Jack Ma's perspective, "Never give up. Today is hard, tomorrow will be worse, but the day after tomorrow will be sunshine," encapsulates the essence of perseverance driven by vision. Believing in the Effort Bank encourages the relentless pursuit of your objectives, regardless of immediate outcomes. As we navigate dark times, the belief that light awaits us keeps us moving forward. Therefore, promise yourself never to give up, trusting that success is inevitable with sustained effort and belief in your vision.

Practicing Jack Ma's "Never give up" philosophy involves embracing resilience, perseverance, and a relentless pursuit of your goals despite the challenges and setbacks you might face. It's a mindset that can be cultivated through various strategies, transforming obstacles into opportunities for growth. Here's how you can start integrating this perspective into your life:

Begin by developing a clear vision of what you want to achieve; understanding your "why" is crucial as it serves as your anchor and motivation during tough times, making it easier to stay focused and not be swayed by temporary setbacks.

Jack Ma's experiences, filled with failures he saw as stepping stones to success, teach us to view failures not as dead ends but as invaluable learning opportunities. This approach builds resilience and enriches our journey with insights and growth by analysing what went wrong and how we can improve.

Persistence is crucial in the "never give up" philosophy, which involves pushing forward even when progress seems slow or non-existent. Breaking larger goals into smaller, manageable tasks can prevent feeling overwhelmed, and celebrating small victories helps maintain motivation.

Being flexible in your approach, much like Jack Ma, who pivoted from his failures to founding Alibaba, is vital; if something isn't working, be prepared to reassess and adapt your strategies while staying focused on your goal.

Surrounding yourself with stories of people who have overcome obstacles and achieved their dreams can provide motivation and lessons on perseverance, and building a support network of friends, family, or mentors who believe in your vision can offer encouragement and advice during tough times.

Maintaining a positive mindset is essential for enduring the ups and downs of pursuing any goal, cultivating gratitude for the journey and its growth rather than focusing solely on the destination, as positivity helps manage challenging periods and keeps spirits high.

Understand that significant achievements often take time. Jack Ma's success with Alibaba resulted from years of hard work, persistence, and overcoming rejections and failures. Mentally prepare for a journey that might take longer than expected but know that persistence eventually pays off.

By integrating these strategies into your life, you're not just adopting Jack Ma's "Never give up" philosophy but also setting yourself up for a journey marked by growth, resilience, and eventual success. Remember, giving up is the only sure way to fail. Keep pushing forward and let each step fuel your journey towards your goals, no matter how small.

Understanding dream stealers is also crucial. These individuals may dissuade you from your path out of jealousy or genuine concern. Recognising their motives helps navigate these interactions positively, focusing on the Effort Bank principle to maintain the pursuit of your goals.

7. Passion

Passion serves as a powerful motivator, driving us towards achieving our goals. While vision might reside internally, within your mind or heart, not visible to others until expressed, passion is immediately observable. Everyone notices the aspect of leadership—it's infectious, recognisable, and capable of being replicated. Passion is critical because it ignites a shared sense of purpose within a team.

When team members observe your passion, they, too, become inspired to act passionately. Oprah Winfrey's words resonate deeply with me: "Passion is energy. Feel the power that comes from focusing on what excites you." This underscores the idea that passion fuels individual motivation and facilitates the duplication of success, a cornerstone of business growth. To foster such duplication, your passion must be evident, guiding others not by mere words but through your actions and enthusiasm.

What then drives your passion? What dreams ignite your excitement? These are vital questions as passion is not just an internal feeling—it's as visible as the clothes you wear. The call to action here is to embody passion and maintain high energy consistently.

It's especially crucial when leading your team; showing them your vigour and dedication encourages them to mirror these attributes. This cultivates a vibrant team dynamic and sets the foundation for achieving collective success. As I often say, the essence of building success in any venture lies in the ability to duplicate what works. Being visible and infectious, passion is pivotal in this process, making it an indispensable element of effective leadership.

The Power of Passion in Leadership and Innovation

Passion is the heartbeat of leadership and personal development, serving as a beacon of motivation and a powerful catalyst for innovation. When imbued with passion, leaders relentlessly push the boundaries of creativity, eager to explore uncharted territories and challenge the status quo.

This relentless pursuit of innovation, driven by a deep-seated passion, propels individuals and teams forward and fosters an environment where breakthrough ideas can flourish.

Moreover, passion underpins resilience, imbuing individuals with the strength to weather challenges and setbacks. This tenacity is contagious and rooted in a passionate commitment to one's goals and visions. It cultivates a culture of endurance and determination, inspiring team members to persevere despite obstacles. The resilience strengthened by passion ensures that leaders and their teams can navigate the challenges of achieving ambitious goals, making it an indispensable asset.

The infectious nature of passion significantly enhances a leader's influence. Leaders who genuinely exude passion for their vision or mission attract and inspire others simply through their energy and commitment. This form of influence is essential for rallying a team, driving collective efforts, and achieving shared objectives. When leaders embody passion, it becomes a powerful tool for motivation, encouraging teams to engage deeply with their work and strive for excellence.

Passion is a cornerstone of effective leadership and personal growth. It motivates, inspires, drives innovation, builds resilience, and amplifies influence. By harnessing the power of passion, leaders can elevate their teams and achieve remarkable success, underscoring passion's pivotal role in leadership dynamics and achieving excellence.

8. Humility

Humility is a virtue that often flies under the radar in a world that sometimes rewards the loudest and the boldest. Yet, its power and value in shaping character, relationships, and societies are immense. Humility is the quality of being modest and respectful, acknowledging our limitations and the contributions of others without seeking the spotlight. It's a grounding force, reminding us that no matter our achievements, we are all human, fallible, and part of a larger tapestry of existence.

Humility plays a crucial role in personal development. It allows for self-reflection and growth, as recognising our imperfections is the first step toward improvement. A humble person is open to feedback and criticism because they understand that their view of the world is not absolute. This openness fosters learning and adaptation, essential for personal and professional development.

Humility forms a cornerstone of leadership attitudes. True leaders, the great ones, embody humility. It's about recognising what we lack and acknowledging our limitations. I've learned that admitting ignorance or uncertainty doesn't diminish respect from others; it often enhances it. Owning up to what we don't know opens the door to acquiring new knowledge and skills. Being humble also means being receptive to feedback and willing to learn and improve from others' perspectives. This isn't about my way or the highway; it's about being open-minded, regardless of your success or position.

I've travelled to over 60 countries, engaging with thousands through public speaking and training, and I've always come away with new insights from the people I meet. This openness fosters personal growth and cultivates a positive team culture.

Humility is often seen as a counterintuitive trait but incredibly effective. Humble leaders are more approachable and relatable, making them more effective at motivating and inspiring their teams. They are willing to admit mistakes and share credit, which enhances their credibility and encourages a culture of accountability and collaboration. By prioritising the organisation's success over their ego, humble leaders foster an environment where innovation and creativity flourish.

Three qualities define humble leaders: coachability, the willingness to admit mistakes, and the empowerment of others. Recognising our shortcomings allows us to address and correct them, fostering an environment where continuous improvement is possible. Humble leaders lift others, showing respect and empathy, which are fundamental to building strong, supportive relationships. This triad of qualities underpins humble leadership.

Societally, humility has the power to heal and unite. Humility reminds us of our shared humanity and fallibility in a world of division and conflict. It encourages dialogue and understanding, helping to bridge divides and build consensus. A humble approach to societal issues can lead to more inclusive and sustainable solutions, as it involves listening to diverse perspectives and valuing collective well-being over individual gain.

Mother Teresa once said, "We cannot do great things in this life. We can only do small things with great love." This resonates deeply with me. Humility isn't about grand gestures; it's about the love and sincerity we bring to our actions, no matter how small. When meeting leaders across various communities and organisations, I value their ability to remain grounded and genuine, reflecting on what makes a leader genuinely humble.

Reflecting on one's humble beginnings is a practice I hold dear. Despite the privileges and experiences I've gained, I will never forget where I came from—a small, obscure town few might recognise. This acknowledgement keeps me grounded. I see myself as a conduit for knowledge, learning from others and passing on what I've learned. Remembering our origins ensures we stay humble, an essential aspect of leadership I cherish.

From novice to master in any field, like the skilled motorcyclist in a video I admire, underscores the importance of humility. Starting from humble beginnings, building skills, and achieving excellence while maintaining humility is a testament to true mastery. It reminds us that success should not lead to arrogance. The journey to expertise—requiring, as some say, 10,000 hours of practice—is about achieving skill and maintaining the humility with which we started. This perspective is vital, ensuring we remain humble, respectful, and always willing to learn as we grow and succeed.

In relationships, humility acts as a bridge builder. It teaches us to listen, value others' opinions, and put their needs before ours. Humble individuals can form deeper connections by approaching interactions with empathy and a genuine interest in others rather than wanting to dominate or impress. This creates a foundation of trust and mutual respect, elements critical to lasting and meaningful relationships.

Despite its quiet nature, humility should not be mistaken for weakness or lack of confidence. On the contrary, it requires strength and self-assurance to put aside ego, recognise our interconnectedness, and approach the world with openness and respect. Humility enriches our lives, enhancing our relationships, leadership, and societal contributions. It's a testament to the idea that the quietest voices are sometimes the most powerful.

9. Service

Service is doing something for someone else without expecting anything in return. This notion lies at the heart of human interaction, enriching both the giver and the receiver. Service can take countless forms, from simple acts of kindness in daily life to dedicated philanthropic efforts to improve communities and societies.

Service takes on a broader meaning. Businesses and organisations often define themselves through the lens of service to their customers, striving to meet their needs and exceed their expectations. This commitment to service builds trust and loyalty, creating a foundation for long-term success. Beyond customer service, many organisations also embrace a culture of service to the community, recognising their role and responsibility in contributing to societal welfare.

As a leader, it's crucial to be ready to assist others. It's about actively taking steps to help and serving as a role model for others. When we help others, and in turn, they help others, it creates a beautiful cycle of assistance. This reinforces my belief in the principle that what goes around comes around. Throughout my life, I've witnessed this first-hand. Whenever possible, I've extended help to those in need, and remarkably, when I've found myself in need, assistance has come, often from unexpected sources, further solidifying my belief in this principle.

One of my favourite quotes from Zig Ziglar encapsulates this ethos perfectly: "You will get all you want in life if you help enough other people get what they want." As leaders, it's our responsibility to embody this spirit of service, offering help without expecting anything in return. Doing so circulates goodwill, ensuring that when we're in need, the universe has a way of providing for us.

The essence of service is to help and then let go without the anticipation of reciprocity, as this can tarnish the purity of our actions and the relationships we build. Practising the ethos captured in Zig Ziglar's quote involves adopting a mindset of service and generosity in both personal and professional realms. Here's how you can integrate this principle into real life:

Active listening is essential to effectively practising this ethic. Truly hearing what others express about their needs, aspirations, and challenges lays the groundwork for meaningful assistance. This initial step is about more than just waiting for your turn to speak; it's about understanding the depths of others' desires and how you might contribute to fulfilling them.

Once you've grasped what others are striving for, the next step is to identify how you can assist. This could involve leveraging your skills, knowledge, or time to help them advance toward their goals. The beauty of this approach lies in the diversity of assistance you can offer, tailored to everyone's unique needs and circumstances. Whether it's lending your expertise, providing a listening ear, or offering practical support, each assistance act is a step toward realising Ziglar's vision.

Offering support without expecting anything in return is a key element of this philosophy. The focus should be on the genuine desire to see others succeed. This selfless approach enriches the lives of those you help and fosters community and shared success. It's about creating an environment where encouragement, support, and positivity flourish.

Furthermore, sharing your resources and connections can significantly impact others' journeys. A simple introduction or sharing of a valuable resource can open doors that might otherwise remain closed. In doing so, you act as a catalyst for opportunity, enabling others to progress in ways they might not have been able to on their own.

Teaching and mentoring represent another powerful way to practice this ethos. By sharing your knowledge and experience, you empower others to grow and achieve their goals. This exchange is beneficial for those you mentor and a gratifying experience that can enhance your understanding and skills.

As you implement these practices, it is crucial to reflect on the impact of your assistance. This reflection allows you to see the tangible results of your efforts and guides you in how to be more effective in helping others in the future. Moreover, practising gratitude for the opportunity to assist others and for the growth you experience enriches your journey, making it more fulfilling.

10. Selflessness

Shifting to selflessness, the Effort Bank elevates service by incorporating the element of sacrifice. While service is about aiding others in achieving their goals, selflessness entails a more profound commitment to benefit someone else, sometimes at a personal cost. This profound form of giving builds trust and loyalty within a team and cements enduring relationships. The joy and satisfaction of helping others realise their ambitions are unmatched.

Abdul Sattar Edhi, a Nobel Prize-winning humanitarian from Pakistan, summed it up beautifully: "My religion is humanitarianism, which is the basis of every religion in the world."

Service is about recognising the needs of others and stepping forward to meet those needs with compassion and generosity. This could be as simple as helping an elderly neighbour with groceries, volunteering at a local food bank, or lending an ear to someone struggling. While they might seem small, these actions can profoundly impact others' lives, offering support, comfort, and a sense of belonging.

My experiences have often involved prioritising the success of others over my immediate interests. This was particularly evident during my time in Bangladesh, where I focused on elevating my team to success before my business endeavours. These acts of sacrifice left a lasting impact, fostering long-term bonds of friendship and loyalty that are celebrated decades later.

These instances highlight that true happiness comes not from self-aggrandisement but from being a catalyst for others' happiness without harbouring any expectations in return. This selfless approach, both in service and sacrifice, epitomises authentic leadership, creating a legacy of meaningful impact transcending time and place.

Ultimately, service is about making a positive difference in the world, one action at a time. Whether through small, everyday acts or large-scale initiatives, service can transform lives and create ripples of change that extend far beyond the initial act. In a world often characterised by individualism and division, service reminds us of our shared humanity and the incredible impact we can have when we come together to support and uplift one another.

CHAPTER EIGHT

LEADERSHIP SKILLS

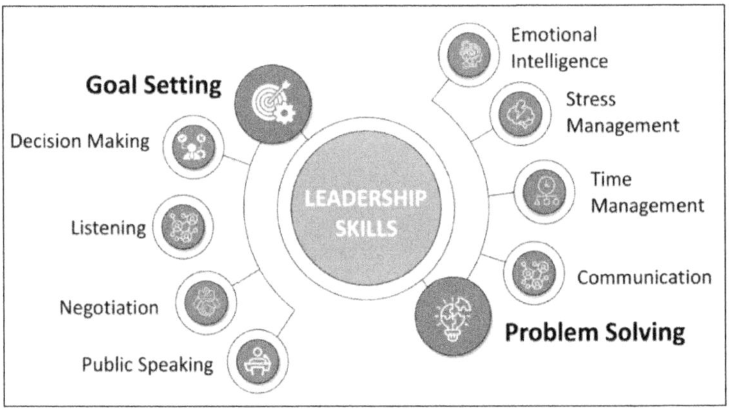

LEADERSHIP SKILLS ARE a set of abilities that enable an individual to guide, direct, motivate, and inspire others towards achieving common goals. These multifaceted skills encompass various aspects of human interaction, strategic planning, and self-management. Cultivating leadership skills is essential for anyone aspiring to lead effectively, as they form the foundation upon which successful teams and organisations are built.

Leadership skills encompass managing stress, time, and resources efficiently. Leaders often face high-pressure situations and tight deadlines, making stress management vital for maintaining clarity of thought and decision-making prowess. Effective time management enables leaders to prioritise tasks, focus on strategic goals, and ensure their team works efficiently towards achieving them.

Perhaps most importantly, leadership skills involve the cultivation of a growth mindset and the ability to inspire others. A leader committed to their continuous learning and development set a powerful example for their team, encouraging them to seek opportunities for growth and improvement. By demonstrating passion, resilience, and a positive attitude, leaders can inspire their teams to embrace challenges, persevere in the face of setbacks, and celebrate successes together.

Transitioning from our broader discussion on the essence and importance of leadership skills, we now connect these overarching principles with the specific competencies detailed earlier. This connection underscores the vital interplay between understanding the theoretical aspects of leadership and applying practical skills in real-world contexts. The attributes such as goal setting, decision making, effective communication, and more, previously explored, serve as tangible manifestations of the leadership qualities we've discussed.

As we explore these ten competencies further, we aim to bridge the gap between conceptual knowledge and practical application, offering leaders a pathway to refine their skills. This approach illuminates each skill's critical role in effective leadership. It equips aspiring leaders with the insights needed to navigate the complexities of their roles and inspire those around them toward shared success.

1. **Goal setting**

Within the Effort Bank framework, goal setting is a fundamental skill for depositing into and withdrawing from this metaphorical vault of potential and achievement. Setting goals is akin to charting a course towards future success, laying down steps and checkpoints that lead to realising one's aspirations. It's about pinpointing what you aim to achieve, crafting a detailed plan, and ensuring these objectives are clear, measurable, and achievable. This meticulous approach to goal setting is a navigational tool that steers your journey through the Effort Bank and ensures that every effort is purposefully directed towards your ultimate destination.

Practical goal setting transforms vague dreams into tangible targets, making the abstract concrete and actionable. It's about breaking down overarching ambitions into smaller, manageable tasks, each acting as a deposit into your Effort Bank. These deposits, over time, accumulate, compounding into a substantial reserve from which you can draw upon to achieve your broader goals. Moreover, each achieved objective brings You closer to your final goal and proves your capability, reinforcing your belief in the Effort Bank concept and your ability to make successful withdrawals when needed.

Practical Ways of Goal Setting

To leverage goal setting effectively within the context of the Effort Bank, consider the following practical approaches:

Practical goal setting starts with identifying specific, measurable, attainable, relevant, and time-bound (SMART) objectives. This clarity fuels motivation by outlining a clear target and facilitates measuring progress, offering a sense of achievement as milestones are reached. Goals can range from short-term daily tasks to long-term career or personal ambitions, each contributing to your life's aspirations.

As you set and achieve goals, you build confidence in your abilities and push the boundaries of what you thought was possible. Therefore, mastering goal setting is about taking control of your life. It’s about making conscious decisions about how you spend your time and what you work towards, ensuring that your actions are aligned with your values, passions, and long-term vision. Cultivating these skills is an ongoing process that can lead to profound personal and professional growth, ultimately leading to a more fulfilling and purpose-driven life.

2. **Decision Making**

In the Effort Bank concept, decision-making is a critical leadership skill, acting as a key mechanism for making deposits into and withdrawals from this potential repository. It is the process through which leaders evaluate various paths, weigh their options, and select the one that best aligns with their and their organisation's goals. This skill hinges on the leader's ability to employ critical thinking, analyse thoroughly, and balance intuition and logic, ensuring that every decision contributes positively to the collective Effort Bank.

Effective decision-making catalyses progress, driving the leader and their team forward on their chosen path. Whether big or small, each decision functions as a deposit into the Effort Bank, incrementally building towards an enormous reserve of wisdom, experience, and strategic insight. This reserve becomes invaluable when faced with future challenges, as it provides knowledge leaders can draw to make informed choices.

Practical Approaches to Decision-Making

To optimise decision-making in the context of the Effort Bank, consider incorporating the following strategies:

Ensuring you have all the necessary information before deciding is paramount. This step involves conducting thorough research, posing questions, and seeking data to shed light on the situation and the potential ramifications of your choices. Once you've gathered this information, the next step is critically evaluating your alternatives. Employing critical thinking, dissect each option to understand its possible outcomes, risks, and benefits while considering both the short-term and long-term impacts on your objectives.

Engaging with your team members to gain insights and perspectives is also crucial. This collaborative method enriches the decision-making process with diverse viewpoints and cultivates a sense of ownership and commitment among the team members towards the selected course of action. While reliance on analysis and logic forms the backbone of decision-making, there are moments when intuition can provide invaluable guidance. If you have a strong gut feeling towards a particular choice, take a moment to ponder why that might be and whether it aligns with your accumulated experiences and knowledge.

Armed with comprehensive information and thorough analysis, you can then decide confidently. It's important to avoid procrastination or indecision, as these can impede progress and result in missed opportunities. Following the implementation of a decision, reflecting on its outcomes is beneficial. This reflective process is precious, allowing you to gauge your decision-making's efficacy and fine-tune your approach for future situations.

Learning from mistakes is an integral part of the decision-making process. Not every decision will lead to the anticipated outcomes, and when results fall short of expectations, it's constructive to view these instances as valuable contributions to your Effort Bank. By learning from These experiences and adapting accordingly, you can apply these lessons to future decisions.

By adopting these comprehensive strategies, you refine your ability to navigate the complexities inherent in leadership, guiding your team towards achievement and success. Each well-considered decision augments your Effort Bank with strategic insights and experiences, enhancing your capacity to make informed choices moving forward. This process underscores a journey of continuous growth and achievement in your leadership endeavours, ensuring that each step is informed and impactful.

3. Listening

Listening is a pivotal leadership skill that transcends mere auditory processing to encompass a deep understanding and empathy for the speaker's perspective. Often undervalued in leadership attributes, listening embodies the capacity to engage with others entirely, fostering an environment of trust, respect, and mutual understanding. Effective listening ensures that leaders not only hear the words being spoken but also grasp the nuances and emotions underlying the message, enabling them to respond more thoughtfully and constructively.

At its core, listening is about creating a connection. It signals to team members that their thoughts, opinions, and concerns are valued and considered necessary. This recognition can significantly boost morale and engagement, encouraging a more open and collaborative team dynamic. By actively listening, leaders can identify underlying issues, anticipate potential conflicts, and gather insights that inform better decision-making and problem-solving strategies.

Practising active listening involves giving full attention to the speaker, avoiding interruptions, and refraining from formulating your response while they're still talking. This requires patience, openness, and a genuine interest in understanding the speaker's point of view. Paraphrasing or summarising what you've heard and asking clarifying questions are excellent ways to demonstrate that you've genuinely listened and to ensure that you've accurately interpreted the message.

Moreover, effective listening extends beyond direct communication. It includes being attentive to nonverbal cues, such as body language, tone of voice, and facial expressions, which can often convey more than words alone. Recognising and responding to these signals can enhance emotional intelligence, a critical component of effective leadership.

Creating a culture where listening is prioritised can lead to numerous organisational benefits. It can improve team cohesion, enhance problem-solving capabilities, and drive innovation by making everyone feel heard and valued. When team members see their leaders as attentive and responsive listeners, it reinforces their trust in leadership. It motivates them to reciprocate, creating a more harmonious and productive work environment.

In conclusion, listening is not just a passive activity but an active effort that plays a crucial role in successful leadership. It's about building bridges, fostering understanding, and creating an inclusive atmosphere where every voice matters. As leaders strive to enhance their listening skills, they pave the way for more effective communication, stronger relationships, and a more engaged and Motivated team, all essential for achieving collective goals and driving organisational success.

4. Negotiation

Negotiation is a critical leadership skill integral to achieving agreements that serve the best interests of all parties involved. It stretches beyond mere compromise to the art of finding mutually beneficial solutions, often transforming potential conflicts into opportunities for collaboration. A leader skilled in negotiation can navigate the complexities of differing interests, values, and goals, steering discussions toward outcomes that bolster team cohesion, project advancement, and organisational success.

The essence of negotiation lies in the balance between assertiveness and empathy. Effective negotiators understand the importance of articulating their needs and objectives while remaining open and responsive to others' perspectives. This duality ensures that negotiations are not perceived as zero-sum games but as opportunities for synergistic solutions that enhance value for everyone involved.

Practically improving your negotiation skills involves a few fundamental approaches:

Preparation is paramount; understanding your goals and those of the other party allows you to enter negotiations with a clear picture of what you hope to achieve and where you might be willing to make concessions. Establishing rapport with the other party is also crucial, creating an atmosphere of trust and mutual respect that facilitates open dialogue and cooperation.

Active listening plays a significant role in effective negotiation. By paying close attention to what the other party is saying and, equally importantly, to what they might not be saying outright, you can identify underlying concerns and objectives that could pave the way to a successful agreement. Asking open-ended questions further aids in uncovering these insights, allowing for a deeper understanding of the other party's position.

Another aspect of becoming a better negotiator is the willingness to explore creative solutions. The best outcomes are often not immediately apparent but discovered through collaborative problem-solving and a desire to think outside traditional parameters. This requires flexibility and a readiness to adapt your strategy based on new information or changing circumstances.

Finally, understanding the importance of timing and knowing when to pause or postpone discussions can be as critical as pushing for an immediate resolution. Some negotiations benefit from additional time to consider options, gather more information, or allow emotions to settle, ensuring decisions are made with clarity and foresight.

In mastering the skill of negotiation, leaders not only equip themselves to deal more effectively with conflicts and challenges but also foster environments where collaborative solutions are the norm. This contributes to the immediate success of specific projects or initiatives and builds trust and respect, enhancing team dynamics and organisational culture in the long term. Developing negotiation skills is not just about securing advantageous agreements; it's about cultivating a leadership style that values and achieves collective success.

5. **Public speaking**

Public speaking is an essential skill for effective leadership. It empowers individuals to influence, motivate, and connect with their audience. It transcends the vital act of conveying information, involving the art of engaging listeners, invoking emotions, and inspiring action. Leaders adept in public speaking can articulate their vision and rally their team around shared goals, amplifying their impact and driving collective efforts towards success.

The power of public speaking in leadership lies in its ability to foster a sense of unity and purpose. Through compelling storytelling, clear messaging, and persuasive rhetoric, leaders can bridge the gap between the present and the future, painting a vivid picture of what can be achieved through collective action. This skill is precious in times of change or uncertainty, where communicating a clear, hopeful direction is crucial for maintaining morale and focus.

To enhance your public speaking abilities, consider the following practical approaches:

Knowing your audience is crucial in tailoring your message to ensure it resonates effectively. By understanding their interests, concerns, and expectations, you can craft speeches that are not only relevant but also captivating. This alignment between your message and your audience's values enhances the impact of your communication, making your presentations more persuasive and meaningful.

Mastery in public speaking is achieved through consistent practice. It is vital to embrace every opportunity to speak in front of an audience in formal presentations, team meetings, or casual discussions. Each speaking experience is a stepping stone in building confidence and refining delivery skills. This continual practice is essential for developing a compelling and assured public speaking style.

Structuring your message with a clear beginning, middle, and end is fundamental for maintaining audience engagement. A well-organized speech ensures that your key points are conveyed clearly and effectively, guiding your audience through your narrative coherently and logically. This structure aids in retaining the audience's attention and enhancing their understanding of the message.

Incorporating stories and real-life examples into your presentations makes your message more relatable and memorable. These narratives can evoke emotions, underscore significant points, and simplify complex concepts, making your speech more impactful and engaging.

Interacting with your audience is vital for keeping them invested in your message. Encouraging questions, fostering participation, and responding to feedback create a dynamic and interactive presentation environment. This exchange makes your speech more compelling and builds a connection with your audience.

Non-verbal communication, including body language, eye contact, and voice modulation, significantly influences how your message is perceived. Developing these aspects through practice can greatly enhance your effectiveness as a speaker, ensuring your non-verbal cues align with and reinforce your spoken words.

Seeking and embracing constructive feedback is crucial for honing your public speaking skills. Input from trusted colleagues or mentors provides valuable insights into your performance, offering perspectives that can lead to meaningful improvements. This feedback loop is essential to your development as a speaker, guiding your efforts to refine and elevate your public speaking abilities.

Public speaking is more than a leadership skill; it's a medium through which leaders can inspire change, foster alignment, and cultivate a culture of openness and engagement. By developing this skill, leaders enhance their ability to communicate effectively and strengthen their connection with their teams, making every speech an opportunity to deposit into the collective Effort Bank and drive their organisation towards shared achievements.

6. Problem-solving

Problem-solving is a pivotal skill within leadership, central to navigating the challenges and obstacles that inevitably arise in any endeavour. It's about more than merely extinguishing fires or addressing immediate issues; it's a comprehensive approach that involves identifying the root causes of problems, generating innovative solutions, and implementing strategies that resolve the current situation and mitigate future occurrences. Leaders who excel in problem-solving can turn challenges into opportunities for growth, learning, and improvement, reinforcing their team's ability to adapt and thrive in an ever-changing environment.

At the heart of effective problem-solving is the leader's capacity to embrace complexity with a clear, analytical mindset. This involves breaking down issues into manageable components, assessing each element with critical thinking, and employing a systematic approach to finding solutions. It's a process that demands creativity for envisioning novel solutions to tough challenges and pragmatism for applying those solutions practically and efficiently.

To enhance your problem-solving skills, consider adopting the following strategies:

Cultivating a solution-oriented mindset is essential in transforming every problem into an opportunity for innovation and improvement. By fostering an environment that encourages a positive approach to challenges, leaders can inspire their teams to focus on finding solutions rather than dwelling on obstacles. This shift in perspective is crucial for maintaining morale and fostering a culture of continuous improvement.

Involving your team in the problem-solving process is invaluable. Leveraging the diverse perspectives, knowledge, and expertise of team members yields more creative solutions and enhances team cohesion and empowerment. Collaborative problem-solving underscores the importance of each team member's contribution, reinforcing their sense of value and belonging within the organisation.

Embracing diverse thinking is fundamental to innovative problem-solving. Encouraging and valuing different approaches to challenges promotes a rich exchange of ideas, leading to more comprehensive and out-of-the-box solutions. This diversity in thought propels teams towards breakthrough innovations and solutions that might otherwise be overlooked.

It is crucial to prioritise and strategise problems based on their impact and urgency. Recognising that not all issues are equally significant allows leaders to focus on addressing the most critical issues first. Developing targeted strategies for these key challenges ensures that resources are allocated efficiently, maximising the effectiveness of problem-solving efforts.

Whether successful or not, learning from the outcomes of problem-solving efforts provides valuable lessons. Reflecting on these experiences helps to identify what worked, what didn't, and why. This reflection is essential to the learning process, allowing leaders and teams to refine their problem-solving approaches and strategies based on real-world outcomes.

Staying informed and adaptive is also critical in the ever-evolving landscape of problem-solving. Keeping up-to-date with new methods, tools, and technologies enhances leaders' problem-solving toolkits, ensuring they are well-equipped to tackle any challenge. This adaptability and willingness to incorporate new strategies and tools into problem-solving ensures that leaders and their teams can navigate the complexities of their work with confidence and creativity.

Problem-solving is an essential leadership skill that significantly contributes to a team's or organisation's resilience and success. By developing robust problem-solving abilities, leaders navigate challenges more effectively and foster a culture of continuous improvement and innovation. This skill is a critical deposit into the Effort Bank, paying dividends through stronger teams, more efficient processes, and enhanced organisational capacity to face whatever challenges come next.

7. Communication

Communication is an indispensable leadership skill for making deposits and facilitating withdrawals from this conceptual Repository of achievements and potential. Communication in leadership transcends the mere transmission of information; it involves conveying ideas, intentions, and emotions clearly and effectively, ensuring that the message reaches its intended audience and resonates with them. This skill is crucial for aligning team efforts with organisational goals, bridging gaps between vision and action, and fostering an environment of trust and collaboration.

Effective communication acts as a multiplier for Effort Bank, amplifying the value of each deposit made through collaborative endeavours. It transforms individual efforts into collective achievements, knitting together team members' diverse strengths and contributions into a cohesive whole. By articulating goals, feedback, and strategies with clarity and conviction, leaders can inspire their teams, encourage open dialogue, and cultivate a culture where ideas flourish. Challenges are met with creativity and resilience.

Practical Approaches to Enhancing Communication

To leverage communication as a tool for enriching the Effort Bank, leaders can adopt the following strategies: Effective communication is a critical aspect of leadership, embodying a balance between speaking and listening. Active listening is foundational, involving complete focus on the speaker to fully comprehend their message, respond thoughtfully, and retain the information shared. This method not only facilitates the collection of valuable insights but also affirms the contributions of team members, showcasing respect and appreciation for their input.

Achieving clarity and conciseness in your communication is essential. Striving to articulate your messages Straightforwardly without jargon or complex explanations helps maintain clarity. This approach ensures everyone is aligned, minimising misunderstandings and fostering concerted efforts towards shared goals.

Tailoring your message to meet the specific needs of your audience is another vital element. Recognising that different listeners may require varied approaches based on their perspectives, knowledge levels, and expectations can significantly amplify the impact of your communication.

Fostering an environment that encourages open dialogue is crucial for nurturing innovation, facilitating effective problem-solving, and strengthening team bonds. By creating a space where team members feel comfortable voicing their ideas, concerns, and feedback, you contribute to a culture of inclusivity and mutual respect.

Utilising multiple communication channels ensures your message is effectively disseminated across your team. Whether through meetings, emails, instant messaging, or internal newsletters, diversifying your communication methods accommodates individual preferences and reinforces your key messages.

Providing constructive feedback is an indispensable tool for fostering growth and improvement. When delivered in a supportive, non-confrontational manner, feedback helps individuals recognise their strengths and areas for development, encouraging them to make meaningful contributions.

Regular reflection and adjustment of your communication strategies are imperative for ensuring their effectiveness. You can significantly enhance mutual understanding and collaboration by seeking feedback from your team on what is working and what isn't and being open to making necessary adjustments.

You can bridge the gap between leadership direction and connection by prioritising and continuously refining your communication skills. Effective communication is the thread that unites individual efforts into a cohesive narrative of success, enabling leaders and their teams to realise their collective potential. This synergy contributes to achieving organisational goals and enriches the Effort Bank, paving the way for sustained achievement and growth.

8. Time Management

Time management is a fundamental skill for effective leadership, integral to maximising personal productivity and guiding a team towards achieving its objectives. It involves strategically allocating time to tasks and activities based on their importance and urgency. By mastering time management, leaders can ensure that both their efforts and those of their team are focused on activities that directly contribute to the realisation of shared goals. This skill is not just about doing more in less time but doing what matters most efficiently and effectively.

Effective time management enables leaders to set clear priorities, distinguishing between tasks that are critical to success and those that can be delegated or postponed. This prioritisation ensures that resources are allocated optimally, enhancing the team's ability to meet deadlines and deliver quality results. Moreover, good time management practices can significantly reduce stress for leaders and their teams by providing a structured approach to workload management, creating a more balanced and productive work environment.

To improve your time management skills, integrating the following strategies into your daily routine can be highly beneficial:

Setting clear goals is the cornerstone of effective time management, requiring you to define achievable objectives that resonate with your vision. This clarity is instrumental in guiding your daily planning, ensuring that each activity is purposefully directed towards your predetermined ends. Incorporating tools like the Eisenhower Matrix helps categorise tasks by their urgency and importance, sharpening your focus on essential functions while minimising time spent on less critical activities.

Allocating specific time blocks for tasks according to their priority enhances the structure of your workday. This structured approach, which includes planning for breaks, significantly boosts focus and productivity. Recognising which tasks can be delegated is equally crucial. Effective delegation liberates your schedule for priorities and fosters team member development and engagement by entrusting them with more responsibilities.

Minimising interruptions is key to maintaining productivity and focus. You safeguard your work's momentum by identifying common distractions and implementing measures to limit them, such as designating times for email checks or setting office hours for queries. Technology and tools, including project management software, calendars, and task lists, are pivotal in enhancing time management and keeping you and your team organised and aligned.

Regular reflection on your time allocation is essential. You ensure more effective time management by evaluating which tasks dominate your day and adjusting your approach accordingly. This continuous process of reflection and adjustment allows you to refine your strategies, ensuring they remain aligned with your evolving goals and priorities. Through these practices, you establish a comprehensive approach to managing time efficiently, fostering a disciplined, focused, high-performing work environment.

Mastering time management is crucial for leadership effectiveness. It's not merely a personal productivity tool but a critical leadership practice that influences the overall performance and success of the team. By effectively managing time, leaders can create a disciplined, focused, and high-performing work culture, significantly contributing to achieving organisational goals and making strategic deposits into Effort Bank that yield long-term success.

9. **Stress Management**

Stress management is an indispensable skill for leaders, pivotal in maintaining clarity, focus, and resilience amidst the myriad pressures and challenges of the workplace. Effective leadership isn't just about driving results; it's also about navigating stress to preserve well-being, foster a positive work environment, and sustain long-term productivity for both the leader and their team. Managing stress is crucial in ensuring that decision-making remains sharp, team morale stays high, and the organisation's overall health is protected.

Leaders' adept in stress management employ various strategies to mitigate the impact of stressors. They recognise the importance of self-awareness and understanding their stress triggers and responses. This awareness enables them to address stress before it escalates proactively. Embracing a mindset of resilience, where challenges are seen as opportunities for growth and learning, helps reframe potentially stressful situations into experiences that contribute positively to personal and organisational development.

Maintaining a healthy work-life balance is also crucial to effective stress management. Leaders set an example by establishing clear boundaries between work and personal time, encouraging their team to do the same. This balance is essential for preventing burnout and ensuring leaders and their teams remain motivated and engaged over the long haul.

Physical well-being plays a significant role in managing stress. Regular physical activity, adequate rest, and a balanced diet are foundational practices that enhance the body's ability to cope with stress. Leaders who prioritise their health improve their resilience and inspire their teams to adopt healthier lifestyles, contributing to a more vibrant and energetic work culture.

Effective communication is another crucial aspect of stress management. By fostering an open and supportive communication environment, leaders can create a space where concerns and challenges can be addressed openly, reducing the potential for stress to build up. Encouraging teamwork and collaboration, where team members feel supported and valued, further alleviates stress by distributing workloads more evenly and fostering a sense of community and shared purpose.

Adopting relaxation and mindfulness techniques such as meditation, deep breathing exercises, or yoga can be incredibly beneficial. These practices help maintain mental calmness and focus, enabling leaders to navigate stressful situations with more excellent composure and effectiveness.

Stress management for leaders is about cultivating a holistic approach that encompasses emotional, physical, and organisational strategies. By effectively managing stress, leaders safeguard their well-being and create a work environment conducive to creativity, productivity, and sustained success. Managing stress effectively ensures that the inevitable challenges of leadership become opportunities for strengthening the fabric of the team and organisation rather than detracting from its potential.

10. Emotional Intelligence

Emotional Intelligence (EI) represents a fundamental aspect of human interaction and personal development, encompassing the ability to perceive, understand, manage, and influence both our own emotions and those of others. This multifaceted skill set is crucial for forging solid and meaningful relationships, navigating the complexities of social interactions, and achieving success in both personal and professional spheres.

At its core, EI involves a high level of self-awareness, allowing individuals to recognise and comprehend their emotional states, triggers, and impacts on thoughts and behaviour. This awareness is the first step in effectively managing emotions, enabling one to respond to situations with a balanced, thoughtful approach rather than being driven by immediate emotional reactions. Such regulation of emotions is essential for resilience, stress management, and maintaining focus and motivation amidst challenges.

Beyond self-management, emotional intelligence extends to empathy and social skills—critical components for building rapport, trust, and effective communication. Empathy, the ability to understand and share another person's feelings, is foundational for compassionate interactions, conflict resolution, and teamwork. It allows individuals to perceive and appreciate the perspectives and emotions of others, fostering mutual respect and collaboration.

The influence of emotional intelligence on leadership and teamwork cannot be overstated. Leaders with high EI are adept at motivating and inspiring their teams, recognising, and addressing the emotional needs of their members, and creating an environment conducive to collaboration and innovation. They are skilled communicators who can navigate difficult conversations tactfully and empathetically, building a culture of openness and trust.

Developing emotional intelligence involves continuous learning and practice. It starts with introspection and a willingness to confront and understand one's emotions. From there, daily interactions require practising empathy, listening, and communication skills. Feedback from others can provide valuable insights into how one's emotional intelligence is perceived and areas for improvement.

Summarily, emotional intelligence is critical to successful interpersonal relationships and professional success. It enriches our interactions, enhances our ability to lead and collaborate, and empowers us to navigate the social world with confidence and compassion. Cultivating EI is a lifelong journey that pays dividends in personal fulfilment and the ability to impact those around us positively.

PART III:

NURTURING

THIS SECTION HIGHLIGHTS aspects of leadership that often go unspoken: Education, one's principles and values, and cultivating an environment where individuals and teams will thrive and flourish in the future. This section shifts the focus from the execution of tasks and achievement of goals to the more subtle yet equally vital role of a leader as a caretaker of their team's potential.

At the heart of nurturing leadership lies the understanding that the success of any organisation is deeply rooted in its members' well-being, motivation, and continuous growth. It's about recognising that leadership extends beyond directing actions; it involves inspiring confidence, instilling values, and encouraging a culture of learning and adaptation.

This section explores the various dimensions of nurturing leadership, from creating a supportive work environment to actively investing in team members' professional and personal development. We discuss the importance of empathy, emotional intelligence, and the ability to connect with individuals on a deeper level, enabling leaders to understand their team's aspirations, challenges, and needs.

Through a series of chapters, we'll examine practical strategies for mentorship, feedback, recognition, and creating pathways for advancement, all aimed at empowering individuals to reach their full potential. This section emphasises the transformative power of nurturing leadership in unlocking the collective genius of a team, fostering a sense of belonging and purpose, and driving sustainable success.

"Nurturing" invites leaders to embark on a journey of reflection and action, challenging them to view leadership not just as a position of authority but as a privilege and responsibility to contribute to the growth and fulfilment of those they lead. As we navigate through this section, the message is clear: the most enduring legacies of leadership are cultivated through the thoughtful, intentional nurturing of talent and spirit within our teams.

CHAPTER NINE

EDUCATING YOUNG MINDS

IN THE GRAND TAPESTRY of life, education stands not merely as a collection of academic achievements but as a cornerstone of personal and professional development. From the early days in Khushab, Pakistan, through the realms of academia to the pinnacle of entrepreneurship, embodies a testament to education's transformative power. Yet, the most profound lessons I've garnered transcend conventional classrooms, extending into the vast classrooms of life and the international stages of business and personal growth.

As a child, I was intrigued that the traditional education system could only partially satiate. The rigorous focus on memorisation and theoretical knowledge often left me pondering the application of complex mathematical theorems to real-life scenarios. It wasn't until I encountered personal, professional development training spearheaded by luminaries like Imran Khan and Ali Khalid that I truly grasped the essence of education. It was an enlightening realisation that education, in its most impactful form, equips us with academic prowess and the attitudes, skills, and insights essential for navigating life's multifaceted challenges.

This exposure was the genesis of my Effort Bank concept—a symbolic repository of efforts, experiences, and learned skills accumulated over a lifetime. Like a financial bank, the more you deposit into your Effort Bank through continuous learning and personal development, the richer your reservoir of knowledge and expertise becomes, ready to be 'withdrawn' or applied when opportunities or challenges arise. This concept underscored my belief in the transformative power of education, extending beyond formal degrees and certifications to encompass the lifelong learning journey we all embark on.

In fostering my Effort Bank, I've ventured beyond mathematics and computer science, delving into the intricacies of leadership, entrepreneurship, and effective communication. Each step of my journey, each roadblock and triumph, has been a learning experience, a deposit into my Effort Bank, enabling me to grow and evolve personally and professionally.

But perhaps the most profound aspect of education I've discovered is its cyclical nature—the invaluable opportunity to pass on the knowledge and insights I've gained. Through coaching, mentoring, and training, I strive to contribute to the Effort Banks of others, helping them unlock their potential and navigate their paths with confidence and clarity. It's a role that brings me immense fulfilment, knowing that each interaction, each shared piece of wisdom, can catalyse growth and transformation.

As I reflect on my educational journey, I am reminded that the true essence of education lies not in the accumulation of degrees but in the continuous pursuit of growth, the unwavering commitment to personal and professional development, and the willingness to share that knowledge with the world. It's a journey that knows no end, a lifelong quest for knowledge, understanding, and the profound satisfaction of contributing to the collective Effort Bank of humanity.

In sharing this narrative, I hope to inspire you to view education through a broader lens, recognise the limitless opportunities for learning that life offers, and embrace the concept of the Effort Bank as a guiding principle in their journeys. After all, the wealthiest bank is not one filled with money but one brimming with knowledge, experiences, and the capacity to make a difference in the world.

Navigating a Disjointed Education System

Around the globe, the education system often presents itself as a fragmented mosaic rather than a cohesive masterpiece. Disparities and inconsistencies abound despite the universal acknowledgement of education as a fundamental right and a crucial pillar for individual and societal advancement. This disjointed landscape stems from various factors, including economic disparities, cultural differences, and policy variations, which collectively contribute to an education system that struggles to meet the diverse needs of its learners.

At the heart of this disjointedness is an economic divide that sees resources and opportunities clustered in areas of affluence while leaving underprivileged regions to contend with scant educational infrastructures. This economic chasm not only affects the physical availability of schools but also impacts the quality of education provided, from the qualifications of educators to the accessibility of technology and modern teaching resources.

Culturally, the global education system faces the challenge of integrating diverse backgrounds and learning needs into a standardised curriculum. Education systems that fail to recognise and accommodate the rich tapestry of student cultures risk alienating learners and perpetuating a one-size-fits-all approach that neglects the nuanced realities of a multicultural student body.

Policy variations further exacerbate the disjointed nature of global education. Educational policies, often dictated by shifting political landscapes, can lead to inconsistencies in educational priorities, standards, and practices. These fluctuations can disrupt the continuity of learning and undermine efforts to achieve a standardised level of education for all.

The consequence of a disjointed education system is a generation of learners who experience education differently based on where they live, their economic status, or their cultural background. This inconsistency hampers individual potential and stifles societal progress, as education is a crucial driver of innovation, economic development, and social cohesion.

Addressing the disjointedness of the global education system requires a concerted effort to bridge economic divides, honour cultural diversity, and stabilise educational policies. It calls for a reimagining of education as a fluid and adaptable process that respects and responds to the diverse needs of its learners, ensuring that every child has access to quality education that prepares them for the complexities of the modern world. Only through such transformative approaches can the education system evolve from a fragmented collection of practices into a unified force for global advancement and equity.

Conventional Education Fails to Teach Us Life.

A prevalent critique of the modern education system is its apparent disconnect from the practical realities of life. While schools and universities excel at imparting theoretical knowledge and preparing students for academic achievement, they often fail to teach essential life skills. This gap between educational curricula and the practical necessity of daily living leaves many graduates feeling ill-prepared for the complexities of adulthood, from managing finances to navigating relationships and fostering emotional resilience.

The core of this issue lies in the traditional focus of education on academic metrics and standardised testing, which, while important, do not encompass the breadth of skills needed to thrive in life. Critical thinking, emotional intelligence, financial literacy, and interpersonal communication are just as crucial as mathematical formulas or historical dates. Yet, these life skills are often relegated to the periphery of educational priorities, if they are addressed at all.

This omission points to a broader oversight within the education system—a failure to recognise that education should be about holistic development, preparing individuals for a career and life. The richness of human experience cannot be captured through textbooks alone; it requires the integration of practical lessons that equip students to face life's challenges with confidence and adaptability.

Moreover, the rapid pace of technological advancement and societal change underscores the need for education systems to evolve, ensuring that students are knowledgeable, adaptable, emotionally intelligent, and equipped with a lifelong learning mindset. The skills needed to navigate the twenty-first century, from digital literacy to environmental stewardship, demand an education system responsive to the changing world.

Addressing this disconnect requires re-evaluating educational values and curricula. Incorporating life skills into the educational framework does not mean diminishing the importance of traditional academic subjects but instead expanding the scope of education to include a more comprehensive skill set. This can be achieved through experiential learning opportunities, interdisciplinary approaches, and a greater emphasis on social and emotional learning.

By bridging the gap between academic knowledge and life skills, the education system can fulfil its true purpose: to prepare individuals to make a living and a life. This shift towards a more holistic educational model promises to cultivate well-rounded individuals prepared to navigate the complexities of the modern world with grace, resilience, and a deep understanding of human experience.

The Mindset Transition from School and University to Work

The transition from the structured environments of school and university into the dynamic sphere of work demands a significant shift in mindset. Challenges often mark this transition as graduates confront the realities of professional life, underscoring the disparities between academic preparation and workplace expectations.

The leap from an environment focused on theoretical knowledge and standardised assessments to one that values practical skills, adaptability, and continuous learning requires a change in behaviour and a profound transformation in thinking.

One of the most striking differences is the shift from a structured, predictable schedule to the unpredictable and often demanding pace of professional life. Students are accustomed to clear guidelines, syllabi, and scheduled evaluations in academic settings. The workplace, in contrast, introduces them to project deadlines, varying workloads, and the need for self-management and initiative. This requires developing a mindset that embraces flexibility, personal accountability, and managing time and resources effectively.

Moreover, the collaborative nature of the workplace necessitates a departure from the individual-centric approach to academic achievements. Success in professional settings often hinges on teamwork, communication, and working harmoniously within diverse groups. This transition challenges individuals to cultivate interpersonal skills, empathy, and a Collaborative spirit, emphasising the importance of contributing to collective goals over individual accolades.

Another critical aspect of the mindset jump involves embracing lifelong learning. Unlike the finite nature of academic programs, professional development is an ongoing journey. The rapid pace of technological advancements and changing industry trends demands a commitment to continuous learning and upskilling. This mindset shift requires recognising that education does not end with a diploma or degree but is a lifelong endeavour crucial for career advancement and personal growth.

The mindset transition from academia to the workplace also entails re-evaluating failure. In educational settings, failure is often stigmatised, associated with poor grades or needing remediation. In the professional world, however, failure is viewed as an opportunity for growth and innovation. Developing a resilient mindset that views challenges and setbacks as learning opportunities is essential for navigating the complexities of the workplace.

To facilitate this crucial mindset jump, educational institutions and employers must work collaboratively to bridge the gap between academic preparation and workplace expectations. This can be achieved through internships, mentorship programs, and coursework that simulate real-world scenarios, preparing students for the nuances of professional life.

As individuals transition from school and university to work, adapting, growing, and embracing new values and expectations becomes paramount. Cultivating a flexible, collaborative, and lifelong learning mindset is beneficial and essential for thriving in the ever-evolving professional world.

Educating Young Minds

When it comes to shaping the minds and hearts of our children, the conventional education system often leaves a gap that we, as parents, strive to fill. Our family's education experience extends far beyond the classroom walls, delving into personal values, resilience, and the profound beauty of curiosity. The essence of our approach is not just about academic excellence but fostering a space where our children can navigate the complexities of life with wisdom, empathy, and a relentless drive for personal growth.

From a young age, my boys are encouraged to embrace a positive outlook, viewing challenges not as insurmountable obstacles but as opportunities for development. This mindset nurtures resilience, enabling them to approach life with a mindset that every experience, good or bad, contributes to their personal 'Effort Bank'—a repository of lessons, skills, and emotional intelligence that will support them in all their endeavours.

Central to our teachings is the importance of never giving up. Whether it's pursuing a passion, overcoming a setback, or striving towards a goal, persistence is a virtue we hold in high esteem. By demonstrating this through our actions and sharing stories of resilience, we aim to instil a sense of determination in our children, showing them that perseverance is often the bridge between aspiration and achievement.

Respect and humility form the cornerstone of our family's values, guiding our interactions with others and our approach to life's many blessings. Nightly reflections on gratitude—where we recount the day's blessings, from the mundane to the significant—instil a deep appreciation and humility in our boys. This practice fosters a grateful heart and a profound understanding that the simplest joys in life are often the most meaningful.

In this fast-paced world, where technology and material success often overshadow fundamental human values, we strive to provide an education grounded in respect, humility, gratitude, and perseverance. Our goal is to prepare our children for the professional world and equip them with the values and attitudes that will enable them to lead fulfilling, purposeful lives. This holistic approach to education is the key to nurturing well-rounded, compassionate individuals ready to impact the world positively.

As we close this chapter, let us carry forward the understanding that education is a lifelong quest of intellectual enrichment, personal discovery, and growth. It's an invitation to view every experience as an opportunity to deposit into our Effort Bank, accumulating wisdom, resilience, and compassion. The true essence of education lies in its power to transform and illuminate paths towards professional success and live a life rich in purpose, understanding, and connection.

CHAPTER TEN

PRINCIPLES & VALUES

PRINCIPLES AND VALUES serve as the moral compass guiding individuals in their actions and decisions. They represent fundamental beliefs that shape one's character, behaviour, and interactions with others. These principles are deeply ingrained and often rooted in personal experiences, cultural influences, and societal norms. Embracing principles and values enables individuals to navigate life's complexities with integrity, consistency, and purpose.

At their core, principles are the foundational truths that govern ethical conduct and define what is right or wrong. They provide a framework for making ethical decisions and navigating moral dilemmas. Honesty, integrity, and accountability are universally recognised and form the basis of ethical behaviour in various contexts, including personal relationships, professional settings, and societal interactions.

Conversely, values are beliefs about what is essential, desirable, or worthwhile. They reflect individual priorities, preferences, and aspirations. Values can encompass various domains, including moral, social, cultural, and spiritual dimensions. Values include compassion, respect, tolerance, justice, and loyalty. These values shape attitudes, guide behaviour, and influence individuals' choices in their personal and professional lives.

Principles and values are dynamic and evolve in response to personal growth, life experiences, and changing circumstances. While some principles are timeless and enduring, others may adapt to new challenges and cultural shifts. Moreover, Individuals may prioritise different values depending on their unique backgrounds, beliefs, and life goals.

Living in alignment with one's principles and values fosters authenticity, meaning, and fulfilment. It enables individuals to live with integrity, pursue goals that resonate with their core beliefs, and build meaningful connections with others. By consciously reflecting on their principles and values, individuals can cultivate a sense of purpose, navigate moral dilemmas, and contribute positively to their communities and society.

Living With Your Conscience

Our conscience acts as an internal compass, guiding us through life's complexities with integrity and authenticity. This section delves into personal anecdotes and reflections on how staying true to one's conscience steers us from regret and towards a life of greater depth and fulfilment. Through these stories, we'll uncover the strength in making choices that resonate with our deepest moral convictions, highlighting the transformative power of living in alignment with our conscience.

Throughout my personal and professional journey, I've learned numerous lessons about values, trust, and resilience. A particularly challenging episode involved a business partnership that generated substantial revenue, around 400 million pounds over five years. My partner and I had distinct roles; I focused on sales and marketing to expand our global presence while he managed the finances. However, a troubling situation arose when, despite our significant sales, we were supposedly running out of money.

Driven by the urgency to address our financial strains, I intensified my efforts, creating incentives, enhancing marketing strategies, and embarking on a global travel spree to boost sales. Yet, the more I contributed, the clearer it became that we were dealing with a leaky bucket scenario. I proposed conducting an audit to identify the leak, but my partner consistently delayed and even obstructed this process. It took me far too long to recognise the signs of betrayal.

My trust in him closed my eyes to the reality of the situation. When I finally looked at our finances, the discovery was shocking. I uncovered personal expenditures, lavish purchases, and under-the-table dealings—all company-funded. When confronted, my partner turned against me, attempting to portray me as the culprit and exclude me from the company we built together. Despite his efforts, his plan was thwarted by my being a shareholder, and his actions required my consent.

The conflict escalated to legal battles across several countries. This experience taught me a harsh lesson about justice and the importance of standing by one's principles. The court eventually ruled in my favour, but the victory was bittersweet, as my partner declared the company bankrupt shortly after, dissolving everything we had built and going into hiding.

This ordeal underscored the value of adhering to one's principles, even when faced with betrayal and injustice. Succumbing to bitterness or revenge is tempting, but true strength lies in remaining true to one's values. The path of integrity may be fraught with challenges, but it is the only way to maintain one's self-respect and principles. Though painful, this chapter of my life reinforced my commitment to living according to my values, undeterred by the actions of others. It's a lesson I deem essential for this book, reminding us that we must cling to our principles and navigate life with integrity in the face of adversity.

Embracing Conscience in Daily Life

Living with conscience requires an unwavering commitment to aligning your actions with your deepest moral and ethical convictions. It begins with a profound reflection on your values, identifying the principles you wish to guide your life. Whether it's honesty, compassion, fairness, or integrity, understanding these core values serves as the foundation of your moral compass, directing your decisions and actions in a way that resonates with your true self.

Making mindful choices is crucial in living with a conscience. Every decision, no matter how small, should be considered for its impact on others and the world. This involves pausing to question whether your actions reflect your values and if they contribute positively to the lives around you. It's about recognising the ripple effects of our choices and striving to ensure they align with the ethical standards we set for ourselves.

Practising empathy and compassion is integral to this journey. Viewing situations through the lens of understanding and kindness allows us to connect with others deeper, ensuring our actions are not just about self-interest but about fostering positive relationships and communal well-being.

Accountability and honesty with oneself are also crucial to living with a conscience. This means admitting mistakes, learning from them, and striving for improvement. It's about having the courage to face uncomfortable truths and the humility to correct course when necessary.

Ultimately, living with conscience is an ongoing process of introspection, learning, and growth. It's about continually asking yourself if you are living in a way that is true to your values and adjusting as needed. By doing so, you craft a life that is not only fulfilling to you but also enriches the lives of others, creating a legacy of integrity and purpose.

Align Yourself with Your Values

Values are the compass that guides our decisions, shapes our actions, and influences our interactions with the world. They are deeply personal yet universally understood principles that offer a blueprint for living a life of integrity and purpose. In the following paragraphs, I will share the core values that have been my north star, illuminating my path through triumphs and trials.

These narratives offer a glimpse into how aligning with one's values can transform challenges into opportunities for growth, leading to a life that is not only successful but also meaningful and fulfilling.

My life experiences have cemented my faith in this idea: nothing you invest in terms of effort is ever in vain. It's a belief that has guided me through challenges and successes, teaching me the invaluable lesson that perseverance and dedication eventually lead to realisation and fulfilment. Belief forms the cornerstone of my philosophy, encapsulated by the concept of the Effort Bank. This principle holds that every instance of hard work, whether immediately rewarded or not, is a deposit into an invisible account of effort, poised to yield dividends in the future.

Belief has been the guiding light through the fog of uncertainty in my life. When confusion clouded my path, especially concerning my education and future direction, my belief in the Effort Bank concept—that nothing is wasted, and that hard work always pays off immediately or eventually—kept me anchored. This unwavering belief that there was a place for me at the top of my field fuelled my journey, ensuring that my steps were purposeful even when the destination was unclear.

Positiveness is another value deeply ingrained in my outlook on life. In any situation, succumbing to negativity is far too easy. However, I've learned that maintaining a positive perspective alleviates stress and opens doors to opportunities that might otherwise remain hidden. This approach has been a beacon during tumultuous times, guiding me towards solutions and encouraging a mindset of growth and optimism—the venture into Bangladesh, armed with hope and an untapped market, blended positivity, and vision. Despite lacking language skills or local connections, a positive outlook and a clear vision assured me that things would work out.

The premature birth of my son, necessitating a hundred-day hospital stay, was endured through positivity. This value was not only my solace but also, I believe, a beacon of hope for him. My faith in the law of attraction and the power of positive thinking was reaffirmed during this harrowing time, showcasing the tangible effects of a positive mindset.

The ethos of never giving up has propelled me through various endeavours, from navigating business challenges to personal trials. This value, instilled in me from an early age, underscores the importance of resilience. It's the refusal to be deterred by setbacks, embracing each obstacle as a bridge towards more significant achievements.

Mental toughness has been a crucial ally, enabling me to withstand the pressures and uncertainties of pursuing ambitious goals. It's a strength honed by confronting and overcoming adversity, fostering a resilience that sustains me through periods of doubt and challenge. When BizNas came to a close, and I faced emotional rock bottom, it wasn't despair that took hold but rather mental toughness. This value, cultivated over miles walked and challenges faced, was my fortress, allowing me to rise from the ashes and pursue further education in the UK.

The betrayal by a business partner and the subsequent legal battles were a harsh test of my mental toughness. Yet, even in the throes of this adversity, I searched for and found a silver lining. I realised that every experience, including this legal ordeal, was an opportunity for growth and learning. It gave me invaluable insight into the legal aspects of running a business, turning a period of strife into an unexpected learning journey. Also, the pandemic's impact on my travel business, just as it reached unprecedented heights, once again called on my mental toughness. This resilience, forged in the fire of numerous trials, equipped me to face this "once-in-a-century" event with a steadfast spirit.

Vision has illuminated my path, providing clarity and direction amidst the complexities of life and business. It's the ability to see beyond the immediate, to imagine what might be, and to pursue that vision with conviction. This forward-looking perspective has been instrumental in shaping my ventures and guiding my decisions. My vision was my compass during the long commutes to university and living within a tight budget. These were not just trials; they were the building blocks of mental toughness. Launching BizNas while working exhaustive hours was a testament to this vision, a beacon that lit the way to something greater than my current circumstances.

Passion drives me, infusing my actions with energy and purpose. It's the zeal with which I approach my goals, the unwavering commitment to my pursuits, and the joy I derive from engaging in work that resonates with my values and aspirations. Resigning from Tianshi to dive back into the direct sales business was driven by passion. The longing for the dynamic energy of direct selling rekindled a fire within me, guiding my steps back into the arena I loved.

Whether through business, personal interactions, or community involvement, the aim to serve and positively impact the world remains a guiding principle. It's a commitment to extending beyond oneself to foster well-being and prosperity in the broader community. Together, these values form the foundation of my life's philosophy, influencing my actions, shaping my goals, and guiding my interactions with the world. They are lessons learned, values cherished, and principles lived by, each contributing to a life rich in purpose and fulfilment.

Crafting Alignment with Personal Values

Aligning with your values is a deliberate journey towards authenticity and integrity, requiring a deep understanding of your core beliefs and principles. This alignment is about making choices that resonate deeply with who you are at your core, fostering a meaningful and fulfilling life. The first step in this journey involves identifying what truly matters to you. Values like honesty, integrity, compassion, creativity, and resilience might emerge. Reflecting on moments that brought you fulfilment or pride can offer insights into your core values.

Evaluating your current lifestyle and choices against your identified values is crucial. This introspection allows you to pinpoint discrepancies between your ideals and your actions. Such an assessment not only highlights areas for growth but also reaffirms the aspects of your life that already resonate with your values.

Setting intentions based on your values is the next step, transforming abstract ideals into actionable goals. Whether in your relationships, career, or personal development, these intentions should be specific and geared towards embodying your values in all facets of your life.

Making decisions aligning with your values is where your commitment is tested. Every choice, from the mundane to the significant, becomes an opportunity to live according to your principles.

Sometimes, this means opting for the more challenging route if it better reflects your values. This process isn't about perfection but about consistently aligning your actions with your values and crafting a life that genuinely reflects who you are and what you believe in.

Positively Impact Others' Lives

This subchapter examines the ripple effect of our actions and how we can foster profound change by aligning our deeds with a purpose beyond ourselves. Through personal experiences and insights, I'll share how the commitment to positively influence the lives of others has not only enriched my journey but has also illuminated paths for those whose lives I've touched.

These values, when earnestly practised, serve as a beacon, not just for our peers but for children, teaching them by example the importance of contributing to the world with generosity and integrity. We'll explore the power of empathy, kindness, and leadership in creating a legacy of positive impact, emphasising that the accurate measure of our lives lies in the difference we make in the lives of others.

My children, aged nine and eleven, often engage in the dramatics typical of their age, declaring every conflict a disaster and vowing silence. In these moments, I introduce the concept of a positive attitude, asking them to find the silver lining in their disagreements. This approach, initially puzzling to them, has become a fruitful exercise. They've started to see beyond the immediate negatives, identifying positives in situations they once labelled disastrous.

Instilling a never-give-up attitude, they've learned to persist in their endeavours, embracing challenges until they've mastered them. Respect for elders is another core value we uphold, alongside humility and the importance of being grateful. We reflect on our day's blessings each night, starting with simple joys like ice cream and chocolate and gradually acknowledging fundamental gifts such as food, water, and a safe home. This practice teaches them not to take life's basics for granted, recognising that many others lack them.

As my children grow, these principles shape their understanding and appreciation of the world. My career once had me constantly airborne, travelling from one destination to another. However, a timely shift has allowed me to spend more precious moments with them, for which I am profoundly grateful. This time has been invaluable in nurturing their young minds and spirits, guiding them through life's lessons with love and wisdom.

Forging a Legacy through Empathy, Kindness, and Leadership

Empathy, kindness, and leadership are not merely attributes but powerful forces that, when wielded with intention and integrity, can transform lives and communities. The journey toward creating a legacy of positive impact is paved with these virtues, each contributing uniquely to the enrichment of others' lives and, ultimately, to the fabric of society itself.

Empathy stands at the core of understanding and connecting with others. It is the ability to step into someone else's shoes, to see the world through their eyes, and to feel what they feel. This profound connection breaks down barriers, builds trust, and fosters an environment where individuals feel seen, heard, and valued. Empathy in action can be as simple as offering a listening ear to someone in need or as complex as developing solutions that address the root causes of societal issues. By cultivating empathy, we unlock the potential for deep, meaningful relationships and community building, laying the groundwork for lasting change.

Kindness, in its purest form, is the unconditional act of giving without expecting a return. The gentle hand lifts others; the warm smile lights up dark days, and the silent strength supports without seeking recognition. Acts of kindness, both big and small, can alter the course of someone's day or even their life. A culture of kindness creates a ripple effect, inspiring others to pay it forward and contributing to a cycle of generosity and goodwill. In a world that often prioritises self-interest, choosing kindness is a radical act that reaffirms our shared humanity and commitment to each other's well-being.

Leadership, when grounded in the principles of empathy and kindness, becomes a catalyst for positive change. Authentic leadership is not about titles or authority but about inspiring, empowering, and serving others. It's about setting an example through one's actions, championing a vision of a better world, and mobilising others to join in the effort. Leaders who prioritise making a positive impact understand that their legacy is not defined by their achievements but by the lives they touch and the communities they uplift. Such leadership does not seek to dominate but to elevate, recognising that the most tremendous success comes from helping others succeed.

The accurate measure of our lives is intricately tied to the difference we make in the lives of others. By embodying empathy, practising kindness, and embracing the true essence of leadership, we forge a path that leads to personal fulfilment and a better world for all. This legacy of positive impact is the most precious inheritance we can leave behind, a testament to a life well-lived and a reminder that the power to create change lies within each of us.

Shaping Lives through Positive Impact Starts at Home

Positively impacting the lives of others, beginning with our children, is a profound and rewarding journey. It starts within the family and radiates outward, influencing communities and the broader world. This process involves leading by example, fostering environments of growth and understanding, and nurturing the seeds of compassion, empathy, and kindness. Here's how one can embark on this path:

Embodying the values you wish to instil in your children is crucial to positively impact them. Children learn more from what they observe in their parents' actions than what they are told. Demonstrating kindness, showing empathy in your interactions, and engaging in acts of service teach your children these values and encourage them to adopt similar behaviours in their interactions with others.

Creating open lines of communication is essential. Please encourage your children to express their thoughts and feelings, listen to them without judgment, and provide guidance that aligns with your shared values. This approach helps build their self-esteem and teaches them the importance of listening and empathy in all relationships.

Encourage acts of kindness and service from a young age. Simple activities, such as helping a neighbour or participating in community service projects, can be powerful experiences. These actions highlight the impact of kindness and the joy of helping others, fostering a sense of responsibility towards the welfare of those around them.

Educate your children about the diversity of the world around them. Exposing them to different cultures, traditions, and ways of life can foster an appreciation for diversity and cultivate empathy. This understanding is crucial in teaching them to respect and value the perspectives and experiences of others.

Celebrate and recognise their efforts to make a positive impact. Whether it's small acts of kindness within the family or more significant efforts in their community, acknowledging their contributions reinforces the importance of these actions and encourages them to continue making a difference.

By starting with our children and extending these efforts to others, we can create waves of positive impact that resonate throughout our communities and beyond. This legacy of kindness, empathy, and service enriches the lives of those we touch and contributes to building a more compassionate and understanding world.

Deep Value Comes from Humility

The profound impact of humility on our lives and the value it brings to our interactions with others cannot be overstated. Humility, often misunderstood as a sign of weakness or lack of confidence, is one of the most vital foundations upon which character and deep value are built. It's a virtue that encourages us to see beyond ourselves, recognise our limitations, and appreciate the strengths and contributions of others. This acknowledgement of our shared humanity fosters an environment of respect, learning, and growth.

Humility is a powerful lesson I learned from Imran Khan, especially evident during our early business conferences and leadership meetings. A moment that stays with me vividly unfolded at these gatherings, where lunch or dinner was served. VIPs are traditionally served first, but Imran chose a different path. Stationed at the beginning of the buffet, he would pick up plates, graciously offering them to each person in line, insisting on eating last. This wasn't an isolated incident; it was a testament to his character, a genuine expression of his humility and service orientation.

This act was inspiring and transformative, challenging conventional expectations about leadership and importance. Initially, it's natural to question such unexpected behaviour and wonder about its motives, given our instinctive lean towards scepticism, a survival mechanism from our earliest ancestors. However, witnessing Imran's consistent display of humility revealed a profound truth about his dedication to serving others, a principle he genuinely embodied.

The impact of Imran's actions rippled through our leadership, fostering a culture where serving others took precedence and where leaders genuinely put their teams' needs before their own. This practice of humility became a model for all, illustrating that authentic leadership is rooted in service. Simon Sinek's book "Leaders Eat Last" echoes this sentiment, underscoring the philosophy that leadership is less about commanding from the front and more about supporting from behind, a concept Imran Khan lived by and inspired in others. Through his example, we learned that the essence of leadership and influence lies not in prioritising oneself but in the humble service of others, fostering a culture of generosity and care.

Humility teaches us that every person we encounter has something valuable to offer, a lesson to teach, or a perspective that could broaden our understanding. By embracing humility, we open ourselves up to these opportunities, allowing us to gain insights and wisdom that would have otherwise been overlooked in the shadow of ego or pride. This openness and willingness to learn cultivate deep value in our personal development and our contributions to the world.

In leadership, humility transforms the traditional hierarchy, emphasising service, collaboration, and the collective good. Humble leaders inspire trust and loyalty, not through authority or fear, but through genuine care for their team's well-being and success. They lead by example, showing that true strength lies in vulnerability, courage to admit mistakes and commitment to personal and collective improvement.

Furthermore, humility enriches our relationships, making them more authentic and meaningful. It allows us to approach others with kindness and empathy, to celebrate their successes as if they were our own, and to offer support in times of need without expecting anything in return. This selflessness, a natural by-product of humility, builds deep and lasting connections with others.

Deep value comes from humility because it shapes us into individuals who contribute positively to the lives of those around us. It encourages us to live with a sense of purpose, to strive for excellence while remaining grounded, and to remember that in the grand tapestry of life, we are but threads interwoven with many others. Humility reminds us that the accurate measure of our worth is not in accolades or achievements but in our impact on the world and the legacy we leave behind.

A Guide to Cultivating Humility

Cultivating the value of humility involves a conscious effort to understand and acknowledge our limitations and strengths and to regard the achievements and worth of others with respect and appreciation. It's a self-reflection, learning, and growth that encourages us to remain open and teachable, regardless of our successes or status. Here's how one can nurture this essential virtue:

Begin by practising self-awareness. Regularly reflect on your actions, motivations, and interactions with others. This introspection helps identify moments driven by ego rather than humility and offers opportunities for growth and change.

Embrace a mindset of lifelong learning. Recognise that no matter how much you know, there's always more to learn from others, regardless of their status or background. This approach fosters humility by valuing the knowledge and experiences of all individuals.

Show genuine appreciation for others' contributions and achievements. Celebrate their successes openly and give credit where it's due. This diminishes tendencies towards envy or competition and reinforces the understanding that everyone has value and something worthy to offer.

Seek feedback and accept it graciously. Whether positive or negative, feedback is a valuable tool for personal and professional growth. Receiving it with openness and grace is a hallmark of humility, showing a readiness to evolve and improve.

Practice gratitude. Recognising and being thankful for what you have and the contributions of others to your life can shift the focus away from a self-centric viewpoint to a more balanced perspective, where humility becomes a natural outcome of gratitude.

Engage in acts of service. Volunteering or helping others without expectation of reward or recognition promotes humility by focusing on the needs of others rather than on oneself. It's a powerful reminder of the interconnectedness of our lives and the joy found in serving.

By incorporating these practices into your daily life, humility becomes an ideal and a living, breathing aspect of your character. It shapes interactions and decisions, leading to a life marked by respect, empathy, and a deep appreciation for the collective journey of growth and learning.

We have examined the pivotal role of education in shaping future generations and fostering positive societal change. From cultivating essential values and leadership qualities to equipping individuals with the knowledge and skills needed to navigate an increasingly complex world, education is a cornerstone of personal and collective growth. By reimagining education as a holistic endeavour transcending traditional classroom boundaries, we can empower individuals to realise their full potential and contribute meaningfully to society.

As we navigate the challenges and opportunities of the 21st century, let us heed the lessons learned from our exploration of education. Let us embrace a lifelong commitment to learning, innovation, and continuous improvement, recognising that education is not merely a means to an end but a journey of discovery and self-realisation. We can create a more inclusive, equitable, and sustainable future for future generations by fostering a culture of curiosity, critical thinking, and collaboration.

CHAPTER ELEVEN

THE FUTURE

REFLECTING ON MY EXTENSIVE travels spanning over 60 countries across five continents, I am struck by the universal truths that connect us all. Despite our diverse backgrounds and cultures, I have realised that beneath the surface, we are more alike than different. Across the globe, people share a common desire to lead meaningful lives, nurture their families, and strive for success.

I envision a world shaped by rapid technological advancements and a shift towards more creative pursuits. With automation reducing the need for manual labour, individuals can engage in more innovative and fulfilling endeavours. The rise of e-learning and the emergence of the metaverse further underscore this trend towards a more digitally interconnected society.

However, amidst these technological advancements, I believe that society's ethical and moral fabric will continue to evolve and strengthen. As access to education and personal development resources becomes more widespread, individuals will be empowered to cultivate their skills and assume leadership roles in shaping a brighter future.

Human Intellectual Development

Human intellectual development is progressing at an accelerated pace, mirroring the rapid advancements in society. With the advent of technology and the widespread availability of information, how we learn, think, and interact has undergone a profound transformation. This evolution is evident in various aspects of our lives, from education to employment and beyond.

In education, traditional methods are being augmented or replaced by innovative approaches that leverage technology and adapt to individual learning styles. E-learning platforms, virtual classrooms, and personalised learning experiences reshape the education landscape, making knowledge more accessible and tailored to diverse needs.

Moreover, the nature of work is evolving as automation and artificial intelligence revolutionise industries and job roles. Routine tasks are increasingly automated, freeing human resources for more complex, creative, and intellectually stimulating endeavours. As a result, there is a growing demand for skills such as critical thinking, problem-solving, and adaptability, which are essential for navigating the complexities of the modern world.

The future is moving more hands-off for humans. Suppose you think about the Industrial Revolution thoroughly hands. But then there was a fear that robots would come in, and now, many factories don't use workers. Anymore. So, the percentage of the population used to do manual physical work, they're not, at least in the West. And it's moving towards the east and south as well. So it'll be less hands-on with more AI development, and we all know where things are moving.

There was a fear at one point. Even people say we will not let our factories become automated because we will lose our jobs, houses, and livelihoods. Other works are being created. Nobody's living off the street. Or at least all those people who were in those factories. There was a fear temporarily, but things happened. There are other ways. New opportunities were created. This will still be the same thing that happened in our case. So, society will be less and less hands-on and more intellectual, at a higher level. We'll have more intellectual discussions in future, and we'll have more, much more meaningful connections and relationships. At that point, you will need more skills, such as human skills. I've been talking about all these keys in this book are human skills.

So, it's setting right into this time and place where we are ready to walk into the future at the pace we are. And then the pace of technology is so fast. The development in the last ten years is much greater than in the previous hundred years. We all agree. The development in the last hundred years is way more than the previous 2000 years, 5,000 years probably. So, the growth in the last ten years has been more than a hundred. Yet the development that will happen in the next two or five years will be way more than the previous thousands of years. So, the following years are significant.

Creativity Skills are Vital

Creativity skills are pivotal in personal development and everyday living, allowing individuals to approach challenges with innovation and ingenuity. In personal growth, creativity catalyses self-expression, allowing individuals to explore their passions, interests, and unique perspectives. Whether through artistic pursuits, hobbies, or entrepreneurial ventures, embracing creativity empowers individuals to tap into their full potential and pursue fulfilment on their terms.

In navigating the complexities of daily life, creativity enables individuals to find innovative solutions to common problems, overcome obstacles, and adapt to changing circumstances. By thinking outside the box and exploring unconventional approaches, individuals can uncover new opportunities for growth, resilience, and self-discovery.

Creativity fosters a sense of curiosity and wonder, encouraging individuals to explore the world around them with an open mind and a sense of possibility. From cultivating meaningful relationships to finding joy in everyday experiences, creativity enriches life's journey and adds depth and meaning to each moment.

In a society often driven by conformity and routine, fostering creativity requires intentional effort and a willingness to embrace uncertainty and vulnerability. By cultivating a mindset of experimentation and embracing failure as a natural part of the creative process, individuals can unleash their creative potential and unlock new pathways to personal fulfilment and growth.

Creativity skills are a luxury and a necessity in today's fast-paced and ever-changing world. By embracing creativity in all its forms, individuals can cultivate a life rich in meaning, purpose, and possibility, creating a legacy of innovation and inspiration for themselves and those around them.

Personal Development Requirements

Personal development is an ongoing journey of self-discovery, growth, and fulfilment. It encompasses various aspects of life, from emotional and intellectual well-being to physical health and professional success. To embark on this transformative journey, individuals must embrace certain fundamental principles and practices that serve as the building blocks of personal development. Here are ten essential requirements for personal development, each contributing to the holistic development of individuals and empowering them to lead fulfilling lives while saving in their Effort Bank.

Self-awareness is the foundation of personal development, providing individuals with insight into their strengths, weaknesses, values, and beliefs. By understanding themselves better, individuals can make informed decisions, set meaningful goals, and navigate life with clarity and purpose.

Setting clear and achievable goals is essential for personal growth and progress. By defining specific objectives and outlining actionable steps to achieve them, individuals can stay focused, motivated, and accountable for their actions, leading to continuous improvement and success.

Lifelong learning is a cornerstone of personal development, enabling individuals to expand their knowledge, skills, and perspectives. Whether through formal education, self-study, or experiential learning, embracing a mindset of curiosity and exploration fosters growth and adaptability in an ever-changing world.

Cultivating emotional intelligence allows individuals to understand and manage their emotions effectively and navigate social interactions with empathy and compassion. Individuals can build healthy relationships, resolve conflicts, and thrive personally and professionally by developing self-regulation, empathy, and interpersonal communication skills.

Resilience is the ability to bounce back from adversity, setbacks, and challenges with strength and determination. By cultivating resilience, individuals can overcome obstacles, learn from failures, and emerge more substantial and resilient in the face of adversity, fostering a sense of inner strength and perseverance.

Effective time management is crucial for personal development. It enables individuals to prioritise tasks, manage commitments, and maximise their time and resources. By developing organisational skills, setting priorities, and establishing productive routines, individuals can maximise their productivity and achieve their goals more efficiently.

Physical health and well-being are essential components of personal development. By adopting healthy habits such as regular exercise, nutritious eating, adequate sleep, and stress management techniques, individuals can enhance their energy levels, mental clarity, and overall quality of life, laying the foundation for long-term well-being and vitality.

Regular self-reflection allows individuals to assess their progress, identify areas for improvement, and gain valuable insights into their thoughts, feelings, and behaviours. By dedicating time for introspection and self-assessment, individuals can cultivate self-awareness, learn from their experiences, and make intentional choices aligned with their values and aspirations.

Maintaining a positive mindset is essential for personal development, fostering optimism, resilience, and growth. By cultivating a gratitude, optimism, and possibility mindset, individuals can overcome negativity bias, reframe challenges as opportunities, and approach life with enthusiasm, creativity, and resilience.

Giving back to others and positively impacting the world is a fulfilling aspect of personal development. By contributing their time, talents, and resources to meaningful causes and serving others in need, individuals can experience a sense of purpose, fulfilment, and connection, enriching their lives and the lives of those around them.

Personal development is a multifaceted process that requires commitment, self-awareness, and continuous effort. By embracing these fundamental principles and practices, individuals can unlock their full potential, cultivate meaningful relationships, and lead lives of purpose, fulfilment, and contribution.

As we stand on the cusp of an uncertain future shaped by rapid technological advancement and societal change, we must embrace the core principles of adaptability, innovation, and collective action. By drawing upon the wisdom of the past and harnessing the power of human ingenuity, we can navigate the challenges ahead and chart a course towards a more equitable and sustainable world. Committing to continuous learning, empathy, and collaboration, we can build a future where every individual can thrive and contribute meaningfully to the global community.

CHAPTER 12

THE HARVEST OF EFFORTS CONCLUDE OUR JOURNEY

As we close the final pages of *The Effort Bank,* I want to revisit and consolidate the valuable insights we've uncovered. This book is more than just a collection of principles; it's a personal conversation between us, reflecting on the profound impact of our efforts in shaping our destinies.

Our exploration began with the simple, yet powerful concept of the Effort Bank, where every endeavour, every struggle, and each act of resilience is a deposit into our future. Throughout the book, I've shared not just my experiences but also universal truths that emphasize how real success stems not from fleeting chances but from persistent, dedicated effort.

Let's recall the narrative arc from the modest beginnings in Khushab, through the ups and downs of entrepreneurship, to the broader applications of the Effort Bank. These stories were not just mine but are now part of your understanding of how consistent effort creates a reservoir from which you can draw strength and opportunity.

We've discussed the importance of not just accumulating efforts but also knowing when to make strategic withdrawals. This means recognizing when to apply the lessons learned from past challenges to navigate current and future obstacles effectively. It's about making choices that align with both your immediate needs and your long-term goals.

As we synthesize the lessons from each chapter, remember that the Effort Bank is a dynamic tool—it adapts to personal aspirations and professional demands alike. It serves as a guide through personal losses, professional setbacks, and the pursuit of goals, providing a structure to manage life's inherent unpredictability.

Now, as you reflect on your own Effort Bank, consider its current balance, think about the investments you've made, and plan how you'll use them to shape your future. The insights from this book are not just theoretical; they are practical stepping stones to a more empowered and purposeful existence.

In closing, I invite you not just to ponder the stories and philosophies discussed but to act on them. Let the concept of the Effort Bank inspire a shift in your mindset—from a focus on immediate results to a commitment to sustained effort. This shift can influence more than just individual lives; it can transform educational systems, redefine professional landscapes, and rejuvenate personal relationships.

Let this book serve as a catalyst for change in your life. Embrace the understanding that every effort, no matter how small, is significant. Keep depositing into your Effort Bank, knowing that these investments secure a more prosperous and fulfilling future.

Together, through the pages of *The Effort Bank,* we've started a movement—a movement that champions effort as the true currency of success. Remember that the journey of effort and reward continues. Each step you take builds upon the last, creating a legacy of resilience and achievement. Carry forward this mantra: your efforts are never in vain; they are the most reliable investments you can make in the ever-fluctuating market of life.

ABOUT THE AUTHOR

ATIF KAMRAN is a highly accomplished businessman and innovative business strategist, having completed his MBA in Digital Innovation from Brunel University London. He was honoured with the prestigious UK Businessman of the Year award in 2017, showcasing his extensive experience in international business. Fluent in four languages, Atif has travelled to over 60 countries, gaining valuable insights and cultural understanding. He is renowned as a sought-after international trainer and inspirational speaker, impacting the lives of several hundred thousand individuals and numerous organizations through his transformative trainings. Atif's core belief in the principle that efforts are always rewarded, whether immediately or in the future, is the central theme of his book, *The Effort Bank.*

Atif's dedication to helping individuals achieve greatness and transform their lives is evident in his work and the impact he has had on countless individuals. With a passion for empowering others, his book, *The Effort Bank,* serves as a testament to his commitment to guiding individuals towards success. Through his innovative business practices and inspirational speeches, Atif continues to make a positive impact on the lives of many, embodying the principles of hard work, dedication, and the belief that efforts are always rewarded in the long run.

Atif firmly believes in the principle that efforts are always rewarded, whether immediately or in the future. This belief serves as the central theme of his book, *The Effort Bank*. He emphasizes the importance of making consistent efforts and investments in oneself, as he believes that every action, no matter how small, contributes to personal growth and success. Atif Kamran's philosophy revolves around the idea that building a strong foundation of hard work and dedication will ultimately lead to achieving greatness and unlocking one's full potential.

Atif's commitment to helping individuals achieve greatness and transform their lives is unwavering. He has dedicated himself to sharing his knowledge and insights with millions of people around the world, traveling extensively to impart valuable lessons through his training sessions and public speeches. Atif's belief in the principle that efforts are always rewarded drives his passion to inspire others to rise above their fears and achieve their goals. His commitment to empowering individuals to unlock their potential and attain greatness is evident in his book, *The Effort Bank,* where he shares practical advice and actionable steps to help others convert fear into freedom.

Atif has created a leadership training program available at www.TheEffortBank.com to further enhance his work of helping other people. This program aims to provide individuals with the tools and knowledge needed to become effective leaders in their respective fields. By offering this training program, Atif is expanding his reach and impact, allowing more individuals to benefit from his expertise and guidance. For more information on this program and Atif's work, interested individuals can visit www.TheEffortBank.com.

Printed in Great Britain
by Amazon

40939693R00158